veggie desserts + cakes

To Marc, for the unwavering support, love and laughs.
To my darling little taste testers, Dax and Polly.
And to my mum, for absolutely everything.

First published in the United Kingdom in 2017 by Pavilion
43 Great Ormond Street
London WC1N 3HZ

Text © Kate Hackworthy, 2017
Design and layout © Pavilion Books Company Ltd, 2017
Photography © Pavilion Books Company Ltd, 2017,
except p.7 © Bill Bradshaw, and pp.12, 21, 105, and
134 © Clare Winfield

ISBN: 978-1-91121-674-2

A CIP catalogue record for this book is available from
the British Library.

10 9 8 7 6 5 4 3 2 1

Reproduction by Colourdepth, UK
Printed and bound by 1010 Printing International ltd, China

This book can be ordered direct from the publisher at
www.pavilionbooks.com

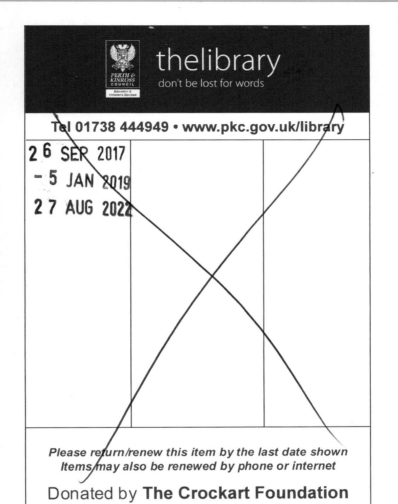

kate
hackworthy

veggie desserts + cakes

carrot cake and beyond

PAVILION

Contents

Introduction

This book isn't about sneaking vegetables into food or disguising them in cake, but instead celebrating them loud and proud as tasty ingredients and making them as much a part of dessert as they are of any main course.

I'm passionate about and inspired by vegetables. These wondrous, nourishing foods that grow all around us are more than salad and much more than something you serve with dinner. They can bring their vitamins, goodness and nutrients to any dish. *And* I can wrap them in cake.

Probably the most familiar dessert made with vegetables is carrot cake, and that shows quite clearly that vegetables in desserts don't taste like main-course vegetables – they taste like desserts. Plus they bring their health benefits and often give a vibrant colour. Vegetables also bring bulk, moisture, natural sugars and nutrients to desserts and mean that less fat and refined sugar has to be added for successful results. Avocado can make a great substitute for butter, root vegetables bring sweetness and, in some desserts, vegetable purée can replace the eggs. The vegetables also give an amazing texture and moistness, meaning the cakes last for days and still taste great.

Just because we're used to having veggies as savoury foods doesn't mean we can't serve them in sweet dishes, too, so it's time to whack them out of the ground and onto the cake stand.

I am unashamedly obsessed by vegetables in all of their glorious hues, textures and flavours. I see no reason why veg and baking can't combine to make more virtuous desserts – or perhaps that should be more sinful vegetables! To me, adding parsnip to a crumble is as natural as adding an apple. Grating squash into a cake seems just as logical to me as using carrot. Because it's sweet, fruit has long been the fresh ingredient added to desserts, but I love the understated sweetness that vegetables can bring. It's now time for vegetables to shine.

How did I start baking with vegetables?
—

Five years ago, coming up to my son's first birthday, I wanted him to have the obligatory birthday cake, but after months of ensuring he ate healthy, fresh foods, I was unsettled about allowing him to indulge in the usual cake. So I started to experiment. After a few trials, his birthday cake was ready: one layer of chocolate and butternut squash cake, and one layer of chocolate beetroot cake, iced with avocado buttercream icing. Now, he might be getting the chocolate and sugar (though less than a normal cake), but at least he'd also be getting a few healthy vegetables at the same time. The cake went down a storm with children and parents alike.

From there, my obsession with vegetable desserts quickly grew, and I became more and more intrigued by the alchemy of replacing traditional cake ingredients with nutritious vegetables. After being frequently asked for my recipes, I began to write about my desserts on my blog, www.veggiedesserts.co.uk. My crazy vegetable cakes and bakes obviously aren't that crazy after all, and the blog quickly began winning awards and gaining international press to such an extent that people from all over the world began contacting me to say that they loved my vegetable desserts. I hope that you will, too.

Now, get your apron and go eat your veg – in cake.

Kate x

On a practical note

Vegetables in this book should be raw, unless specified otherwise.

Although this book is about baking with vegetables, I've included recipes using beans and fruits, such as avocado and cucumber. They're normally used in savoury dishes, so I wanted to show how versatile they are in sweet treats.

Fresh produce can be temperamental. Factors such as freshness and seasonality can affect the colour of the final result, but it should still taste great. Go for the freshest veg you can for a more vibrant colour.

Adding vegetables to cake batter can sometimes make it split, but don't worry as the results will be fine. Just add a tablespoon of flour and gently mix again.

Most of my recipes have a bit of extra vanilla in them. This is a trick that allows you to use less sugar, but keeps the sweetness.

A note on blitzing – to get the brightest vegetable colours in a cake, when it calls for purée, you'll need to purée it well. I usually use a hand-held blender. I've had pricey ones and not-so-pricey ones, and I've found that sometimes the cheapest ones have done the best job of turning veg into a paste. Kale is definitely the most difficult veg to purée as it's so fibrous, but persevere for a bright green cake. For finely chopped and grated hard vegetables, I like to use a mini food processor. The smaller bowl means you spend far less time scraping down the sides.

Many vegetables, even puréed, can have a varying water content, so watch the bake towards the end of the cooking time and check for doneness with a skewer.

Cakes

Kale and Apple Cake with Apple Icing

Serves 12

For the cake
—

200g/7oz/6½ packed cups
  fresh kale leaves, woody
  stalks discarded
3 large free-range eggs
100ml/3½fl oz/scant ½ cup
  vegetable oil
2 tsp vanilla extract
100g/3½oz/½ cup apple
  sauce (see tip on p.12)
175g/6¼oz/heaped ¾ cup
  granulated sugar
2 eating (dessert) apples,
  peeled and grated
250g/9oz/2 cups plain
  (all-purpose) flour

2 tsp baking powder
½ tsp salt
butter, or non-stick cooking
  spray, for greasing

For the apple icing
—

2 tbsp unsalted butter,
  softened
2 tbsp smooth apple sauce
250g/9oz/1¾ cups plus 1 tbsp
  icing (confectioners') sugar
½ tsp vanilla extract

To decorate
—

1 handful of blueberries
  (optional)

This is the most popular vegetable cake on my blog, with countless readers making it time and again. Kale has risen up the ranks to become the world's trendiest leafy green, but I've shunned the usual kale chips and smoothies, and made it naughty by baking it into a cake. It has a delicate apple-flavoured sponge, topped with a zesty apple icing and, although there is quite a bit of kale, the flavour doesn't overpower the other ingredients.

I've found that the fresher the kale, the brighter the colour of the cake. When I can get my hands on freshly picked local heads of kale, the green is incredibly vibrant. Supermarket bags of chopped kale also work fine, but the colour can occasionally turn out a little less bright. But don't be tempted to add more kale to make the colour brighter or its flavour will come through too much!

To make the cake

Preheat the oven to 180°C/160°C fan/350°F/gas 4. Grease and line two 20cm/8in round cake pans.

Tear the kale leaves into bite-sized pieces and boil or steam them for a few minutes until tender. Refresh by running under cold water to cool, then drain, squeeze out any excess moisture and purée well with a hand blender. Kale is one of the more difficult vegetables to purée, since it's quite fibrous, and I've found a hand blender works best. Persevere for a few minutes to blitz the fibrous leaves to a paste, though it will still be slightly stringy. Set aside.

In a large bowl, beat the eggs, oil, vanilla, apple sauce and sugar together with an electric mixer. Beat in the kale purée and grated apple. Sift in the flour, baking powder and salt, then gently combine.

Divide the mixture between the prepared pans and bake for 30 minutes, or until a skewer inserted in the middle comes out clean.

Leave to cool in the pans for 5 minutes, then turn out onto a wire rack to cool completely.

Continued

Tip
—

In both the icing and cake, apple sauce replaces some of the fat and sugar, lightening the texture. If your apple sauce has chunks, it's fine for the cake, but is best completely smooth for the icing, so purée it with a hand blender. If you don't have apple sauce, just peel, core and slice 4 apples, steam until soft, then purée with a hand blender, then measure out the amounts needed in the recipe.

To make the apple icing

In a large bowl, beat the butter and apple sauce with an electric mixer. Add the remaining icing ingredients and beat until smooth. If necessary, add a little more icing sugar or a teaspoon of milk to reach the consistency of thick frosting. Store in the fridge until ready to use.

Sandwich the cakes together with about a quarter of the icing, then spread the remaining icing over the top and sides of the cooled cake. Top with the blueberries to finish.

Beetroot Chocolate Bundt Cake with Earl Grey Icing

Serves 12

For the cake
—

200g/7oz/1 cup cooked
   beetroot (roasted, boiled
   or steamed, see tip on p.14)
100g/3½oz/generous ⅓ cup
   plain full-fat yogurt
100ml/3½fl oz/scant
   ½ cup vegetable oil
150g/5¼oz/¾ cup
   granulated sugar
3 large free-range eggs
2 tsp vanilla extract
250g/9oz/2 cups plain
   (all-purpose) flour
60g/2oz/scant ⅔ cup
   unsweetened cocoa powder

2 tsp baking powder
½ tsp bicarbonate of soda
   (baking soda)
½ tsp salt
butter or non-stick
   cooking spray

For the Earl Grey icing
—

4 tbsp double (heavy) cream
2 Earl Grey tea bags
180g/6¼oz/generous 1¾ cups
   icing (confectioners') sugar
2–3 tsp warm water, to thin

To decorate
—

2 handfuls of mixed berries

A bundt cake looks so retro, so regal. It sits on the serving plate like a sponge crown, its intricate silhouette determined by your choice of pan. One of the great things about the ornate shape is that you need only a little bit of icing to decorate it beautifully. The sponge of this cake is springy and light, with a decadent fudgy chocolate taste that pairs well with the subtle earthiness of beetroot. I've infused the icing with Earl Grey, so you can have your cup of tea and slice of cake in one. The tea's bergamot and citrus notes give a subtle flavour to complement the rich chocolate cake as the icing slides down the bundt cake's ridges. The best decoration for this cake is a garland of fruit, because there are no sprinkles or sparkles as beautiful as fresh berries.

To make the cake
Preheat the oven to 180°C/160°C fan/350°F/gas 4. Grease a 20cm/8in bundt pan with butter or non-stick cooking spray.

Purée the beetroot with a hand blender and set aside.

In a large bowl, beat the yogurt, oil and sugar together with an electric mixer. Add the eggs, one at a time, and beating each one in well. Stir in the puréed beetroot with the vanilla.

Sift in the flour, cocoa, baking powder, bicarbonate of soda and salt, then gently mix until combined.

Pour into the prepared pan and bake for 50–60 minutes, or until a skewer inserted in the middle comes out clean.

Leave to cool in the pan for 10 minutes, then turn out onto a wire rack to cool completely.

Continued

You can make this cake with any cooked beetroot, such as leftover roasted or boiled beets, and for ease you can even use the vacuum-packed ones found in most supermarkets, but be sure to get the type that isn't packed in vinegar.

To make the Earl Grey icing

Gently warm the cream in a small pan, then remove from the heat and add the tea bags. Allow the tea to steep in the warm cream for 5 minutes, swirling the cream in the pan occasionally.

Remove the tea bags and gently squeeze out any cream from them back into the pan, taking care not to split the bags open. Leave to cool completely.

Sift the icing sugar into the cream and whisk until smooth, adding enough warm water, a teaspoon at a time, to thin to a thick drizzling consistency. Drizzle over the completely cooled bundt cake, down the ridges, then top with the mixed berries.

Carrot Victoria Sponge with Carrot Jam

Serves 8

For the carrot jam
Makes 700g/1lb 9oz/2⅓ cups
(2–3 jam jars)
—
750g/1lb 10oz carrots, peeled
450g/1lb/2 cups granulated
 sugar
zest of 1 lemon
juice of 2 lemons

For the cake
—
100g/3½oz carrot
 (about 1 medium carrot)

150g/5¼oz/⅔ cup unsalted
 butter, softened, plus extra
 for greasing
115g/4oz/½ cup caster
 (superfine) sugar
2 large free-range eggs
2 tsp vanilla extract
200g/7oz/1⅔ cups plain
 (all-purpose) flour
2 tsp baking powder
½ tsp salt

For the filling and decoration
—
150ml/5fl oz/scant ⅔ cup
 double (heavy) cream
about 2 tbsp caster
 (superfine) sugar

Carrot cakes have long been wintery, spiced affairs with lots of oil and cinnamon, but I also like to use carrots in lighter desserts. Here, I've put finely grated carrot into the batter of a classic Victoria sponge, giving extra natural sweetness and an orange colour to this airy cake.

I've sandwiched the layers together with a simple three-ingredient carrot jam, which is based on a recipe from *Mrs Beeton's Book of Household Management* (1865). It's really easy to make, luminously bright orange and, oddly, tastes just like apricot jam. It adds a great flavour to the cake, plus you'll have loads left over for spreading on toast at breakfast. You should always use sterilized jars, and the easiest way to sterilize them is to run them through the dishwasher and use them hot and dry when the cycle has finished. The carrot jam can be substituted with apricot jam.

To make the carrot jam
Grate one of the peeled carrots so you have 50g/2oz/⅓ cup of grated carrot. Set aside. Chop the rest of the carrots into rounds, then place them in a saucepan with enough cold water to just cover them. Bring to the boil, then cook over a medium heat for about 10 minutes until soft. Drain, then purée the carrots with a hand blender (or in a food processor). Put the puréed carrots into a sieve (fine-mesh strainer) and press out, and discard, any excess water.

Weigh out 400g/14oz of puréed carrot (see Tip on p.18 on how to use the rest).

Put the purée and the 50g/2oz/⅓ cup of grated carrot into a large saucepan over a medium heat. Add the sugar, bring to the boil, and boil for 5 minutes, stirring constantly. Skim off and discard any froth that rises to the top.

Allow the jam to cool slightly, then stir in the lemon zest and juice. Pour into sterilized, lidded jars, seal, and leave to cool, then refrigerate.

Continued

Any leftover carrot purée from the jam can be mixed with a little maple syrup and cinnamon, then used as a topping for porridge or yogurt.

To make the cake
Preheat the oven to 190°C/170°C fan/375°F/gas 5. Grease two 15cm/6in round cake pans and line the bases with baking parchment.

Peel and finely grate the carrots or whiz in a food processor until finely chopped, then set aside.

In a large bowl, cream together the butter and sugar with an electric mixer until pale and fluffy. Add the eggs, one at a time and beating each one in well, then stir in the carrot and vanilla. Sift in the flour, baking powder and salt, and fold in gently to combine.

Divide the batter between the prepared cake pans and bake for 20 minutes, or until golden and the centre springs back when touched.

Leave to cool in the pans for 5 minutes, then turn out onto a wire rack to cool completely.

To finish
Beat the cream with about 2 teaspoons of sugar together until thick.

When the cakes are completely cool, sandwich them together with 2–3 tablespoons of carrot jam and the cream, then lightly dust the top with the remaining caster sugar.

Pumpkin Cheesecake

Serves 10

For the base
—

200g/7oz/2 cups digestive
  biscuits (Graham crackers)
85g/3½oz/⅓ cup unsalted
  butter, melted

For the filling
—

3 x 225g/8oz packages
  soft cheese, at room
  temperature

425g/15oz can of
  pumpkin purée
200g/7oz/1 cup caster
  (superfine) sugar
4 tbsp crème fraîche
  (sour cream)
2 tbsp plain (all-purpose) flour
4 large free-range eggs
1 tsp vanilla extract
½ tsp ground cinnamon
¼ tsp ground ginger

This pumpkin cheesecake is rich, gently spiced and as smooth as silk. Cheesecakes can be a little finicky, and sometimes the top cracks, or it might sink a little. But don't panic – it will still taste amazing. Just follow the instructions to the letter, make sure that the ingredients are at room temperature and don't overbeat the mixture. You just want to mix it and make it smooth, not whip in loads of air. This cheesecake needs time and patience, but it's completely worth it. I've based my recipe on US chef Paula Deen's classic, because if there are two things Americans know about, it's pumpkin and cheesecake.

Tip
—

Not all cheesecake recipes call for pre-baking the crust, but I recommend that you do. After years of watching baking shows on the telly, we've all learned that nobody likes a soggy bottom.

To make the base

Preheat the oven to 170°C/150°C fan/350°F/gas 4. Make sure all the ingredients are at room temperature.

Crush the digestive biscuits and place them into a large bowl, then pour in the melted butter and mix well. Press the mixture evenly over the base of a 23cm/9in round springform cake pan.

Bake the base for 10 minutes, then remove from the oven and set aside. Leave the oven on.

To make the filling

In a large bowl, beat the soft cheese with an electric mixer on medium/low until smooth. Add the pumpkin purée, sugar, crème fraîche and flour, and continue mixing until smooth. Add the eggs, cinnamon, vanilla and ginger, and beat on medium/low until completely combined, then continue mixing for about 1 minute more. Be sure to scrape down the sides of the bowl during mixing to make sure that it is all completely combined.

Pour the mixture over the base and bake for 60 minutes, or until the top is slightly browned and the centre is set and risen but still slightly jiggly.

Remove it from the oven and allow to come to room temperature, then refrigerate overnight, or until thoroughly chilled. It will continue to set until cool.

Root Vegetable Cake with Whipped Tahini Icing

Serves 14

For the cake
—

200g/7oz mixed root veg, such as carrot, parsnip, etc., peeled (use peelings if organic)
3 large free-range eggs
120ml/4fl oz/½ cup maple syrup or honey
120ml/4fl oz/½ cup vegetable oil
120g/4oz/½ cup plain Greek yogurt
2 tsp vanilla extract
150g/5¼oz/1 cup raisins
200g/7oz/1⅔ cups plain wholemeal flour

2 tsp baking powder
1 tsp bicarbonate of soda (baking soda)
2 tsp ground cinnamon
1 tsp freshly grated nutmeg
1 tsp ground ginger
½ tsp salt
butter, for greasing

For the whipped tahini icing
—

50g/1¾oz/¼ cup unsalted butter, softened
1½ tbsp tahini
200g/7oz/1⅔ cups icing (confectioners') sugar
½ tsp vanilla extract
1–2 tsp milk (if necessary)

This is a great way to use up any leftover root veg, including carrots, parsnips and beetroot, and even turnip or swede (rutabaga). Each vegetable brings a different, earthy sweetness, and all work well within the spiced sponge. You can use a single type of vegetable or a mix of whatever you have to hand. If using organically grown veg for your Sunday roast, you can save the washed peelings and finely grate them for this cake – it's a great way to reduce food waste.

I've used maple syrup instead of sugar and replaced half of the oil with yogurt, making it a bit lighter than a typical carrot cake.

Tip
—

Tahini is a sesame seed paste, similar to nut butters, and is widely available. It has a lovely strong, dry taste and a mild bitterness that balances out the sweetness of the icing.

To make the cake
Preheat the oven to 180°C/160°C fan/350°F/gas 4. Grease a 23cm/9in round cake pan and line the base with baking parchment. Whiz the root veg in a food processor until finely grated. Set aside.

In a large bowl, beat the eggs, maple syrup/honey, oil, yogurt and vanilla with an electric mixer, until thoroughly mixed.

Stir in the grated root vegetables and the raisins.

Sift the flour, baking powder, bicarbonate of soda, cinnamon, nutmeg, ginger and salt into the mixture (adding any sieved-out bran back into the bowl), and gently combine.

Pour into the prepared pan, level to the edges and bake for 40–50 minutes, or until a skewer inserted in the middle comes out clean. Leave to cool in the pan for 15 minutes, then turn out onto a wire rack to cool completely.

To make the whipped tahini icing
In a large bowl, beat the butter and tahini together with an electric mixer. Add the icing sugar and vanilla, and beat until light and fluffy. If necessary, add more icing sugar or a teaspoon of milk to reach the consistency of thick frosting. Spread over the completely cooled cake.

Pea and Vanilla Cake with Lemon Icing

Serves 8

For the cake
—

275g/10oz/1¾ cups fresh
  or frozen peas
200g/7oz/generous ¾ cup
  unsalted butter, softened,
  plus extra for greasing
150g/5¼oz/¾ cup
  granulated sugar
3 large free-range eggs
2 tsp vanilla extract
zest and juice of ½ lemon
250g/9oz/2 cups plain
  (all-purpose) flour

2 tsp baking powder
½ tsp salt

For the lemon buttercream
—

150g/5¼oz/⅔ cup unsalted
  butter, softened
300g/10½oz/2½ cups icing
  (confectioners') sugar
zest and juice of ½ lemon

To finish
—

pea shoots (optional)
lemon zest (optional)

This sweet pea cake tastes like a vanilla sponge, but with added goodness from the peas and a lovely pastel green colour. You can use fresh peas when in season, but it also works perfectly well with frozen ones. The cake is enrobed in a zingy lemon icing to enliven the flavour and looks lovely decorated with a halo of pea shoots and a sprinkling of lemon zest.

Although peas certainly aren't your usual cake ingredient, do trust me on this one – in all the times I've made this, nobody has ever guessed that the gentle sweetness and beautiful colour comes from humble garden peas.

To make the cake

Preheat the oven to 170°C/150°C fan/325°F/gas 3. Grease and line three 15cm/6in round cake pans.

Boil the peas for a few minutes, drain, refresh under cold water and drain again. Purée with a hand blender until smooth. Set aside.

In a large bowl, cream the butter and sugar with an electric mixer until light and fluffy. Beat in the eggs well, one at a time, then beat in the cooled pea purée, vanilla, lemon zest and juice. Sift in the flour, baking powder and salt, and stir gently to combine.

Divide the batter among the prepared pans, then bake for 25 minutes, or until a skewer inserted in the middle comes out clean. Leave to cool in the pans for 10 minutes, then turn out onto a wire rack to cool completely before icing.

To make the lemon buttercream

In a large bowl, cream the butter with an electric mixer until fluffy. Add the icing sugar and beat until combined. Beat in the lemon zest and a little of the juice. If necessary, add more icing sugar or a teaspoon of milk to reach the consistency of thick frosting. Store in the fridge until ready to use.

Sandwich together the cake layers with a little of the buttercream. Cover the cake in the remaining buttercream and decorate with pea shoots and lemon zest.

Pear and Parsnip Cake with Salted Honey Buttercream and Chocolate Ganache

Serves 12

100g/3½oz raw peeled parsnip (approx. 1 medium parsnip)
2 ripe pears
225g/8oz/1 cup unsalted butter, softened
150g/5¼oz/¾ cup caster (superfine) sugar
4 large free-range eggs
2 tsp vanilla extract
225g/8oz/heaped 1¾ cup self-raising flour
2 tsp baking powder
½ tsp salt

For the salted honey buttercream
—
120g/4¼oz/½ cup unsalted butter, softened
500g/18oz/4 cups icing (confectioners') sugar
4 tbsp clear honey
4 tbsp milk
½ tsp sea salt

For the chocolate ganache
—
100ml/3½fl oz/scant ½ cup double (heavy) cream
100g/3½oz good-quality dark chocolate, chopped

My favourite cake growing up was a pear and chocolate cake that I often requested from my mum for my birthday. The recipe for that cake has long been lost, but I love bringing those memorable flavours back together, this time with the unusual, but welcome, addition of sweet parsnip.

I love the fluffy and cloud-like texture of this cake. The parsnip subtly sweetens the airy sponge while the pears bring flavour and their delicate perfume. I've covered the cake in a salted honey buttercream to bring more complex flavours, then drizzled the sides with a dark chocolate ganache. As the cake has these two icings, I've lowered the sugar content of the cake somewhat so it isn't overly sweet.

To make the cake
Preheat the oven to 180°C/160°C fan/350°F/gas 4. Grease three 20cm/8in cake pans and line the bases with baking parchment.

Finely grate the parsnip or whiz in a food processor until fine, then set aside. Peel, core and finely dice the pears.

In a large bowl, cream the butter and sugar with an electric mixer until pale and fluffy. Beat in the eggs, one at a time, beating well after each addition, then stir in the parsnip, pears and vanilla.

Sift in the flour, baking powder and salt, and stir gently to combine.

Divide the batter between the prepared pans and bake for 20 minutes, or until golden and the centre springs back when touched.

Leave to cool in the pans for 5 minutes, then turn out onto a wire rack to cool completely.

Continued

To make the salted honey buttercream
In a large bowl, beat the butter with an electric mixer until smooth, then add the honey and beat well. Add the icing sugar and milk, then beat until smooth. Stir in the salt.

Divide the buttercream into two bowls and save one for the final coat of icing. Using one of the bowls, spread a little icing between each layer, right to the edge, and sandwich together. Spread a little more icing on the very top and sides to create a 'crumb coat' icing layer. It won't cover it entirely, but will make it smooth and stop the final layer getting messy with cake crumbs. Chill the cake for 30 minutes to firm up the crumb coat.

Carefully apply the second bowl of buttercream to create the final layer of icing over the top and sides. Using a palette knife, smooth it completely around the cake. Chill the cake for 45 minutes before finishing with the ganache.

To make the chocolate ganache
Heat the cream in a saucepan just to the boiling point. Remove from the heat and stir in the chopped chocolate. Allow it to stand for 2 minutes before beating it until smooth. Set aside for 10 minutes to cool to room temperature.

Remove the cake from the fridge and spoon a teaspoon of the ganache at a time over the top edge and encourage it to drip down the side decoratively. Repeat all the way round the cake, then fill the top with ganache.

Carrot and Pineapple Polenta Cake with Pineapple Drizzle

Serves 12

For the cake
—

100g/3½oz carrot
  (1 medium carrot), peeled
200g/7oz pineapple flesh,
  fresh or canned, drained
  (juice reserved for drizzle)
150g/5¼oz/⅔ cup unsalted
  butter, softened, plus extra
  for greasing
125g/4½oz/⅔ cup caster
  (superfine) sugar
3 large free-range eggs

100g/3oz/½ cup polenta
  or fine cornmeal
  (not quick-cook polenta)
200g/7oz/1⅔ cups ground
  almonds
1½ tsp baking powder
  (check that it's gluten-free,
  if required)
zest and juice of ½ lemon
1 tsp vanilla extract

For the pineapple drizzle
—

3–4 tsp pineapple juice
6 tbsp icing (confectioners')
  sugar

This naturally gluten-free cake has a pleasant rustic texture from the polenta and ground almonds, while the pineapple and carrot beautifully permeate it with their natural juices. It's a delightfully tender, dense and crumbly cake that's really easy to make: you just put all the ingredients into one bowl and mix. Simple. It's finished with a sweet pineapple drizzle for a lively citrus accent.

To make the cake
Preheat the oven to 180°C/160°C fan/350°F/gas 4. Grease a 23cm/9in loose-bottomed or springform cake pan and line the base with baking parchment.

Peel and finely grate the carrot, or chop and whiz in a food processor until fine. Set aside.

Finely chop the pineapple, reserving the juice.

In a large bowl, beat the carrot and pineapple with all remaining cake ingredients until well combined. Pour the mixture into the prepared pan and spread out evenly.

Cook for 50–60 minutes until the surface is lightly brown and the cake pulls away slightly from the sides of the tin.

Allow the cake to cool completely in the pan before carefully turning out.

To make the pineapple drizzle
Stir the pineapple juice and icing sugar together until smooth. Drizzle over the completely cooled cake and serve.

Courgette and Poppy Seed Loaf with Lavender Glaze

Serves 8–10

For the cake
—

200g/7oz courgettes
  (zucchini)
125g/4½oz/½ cup unsalted
  butter, softened, plus extra
  for greasing
125g/4½oz/⅔ cup caster
  (superfine) sugar
2 large free-range eggs
2 tbsp lemon juice
1 tbsp lemon zest

175g/6oz/heaped 1⅓ cups
  self-raising flour
1½ tbsp poppy seeds

For the lavender glaze
—

3 tbsp lemon juice
1½ tsp culinary lavender
125g/4½oz/1 cup icing
  (confectioners') sugar

To decorate (optional)
—

1 tsp culinary lavender
twists of lemon

When I tell people about my passion for baking with vegetables, they usually ask me if I grow my own veg, to which I have to grudgingly admit that I am a terrible gardener. I lived on a houseboat in London for many years, and I put my lack of gardening success down to swans nibbling my plants and the difficulty of growing vegetables in containers, but really the problem was that I was neglectful. The plants punished me for being remiss and refused to produce the bounties I'd dreamt of at the garden centre. Now that I have a garden, I've tried again to grow veg, but so far I've just created a feast for slugs and snails, much to my frustration.

Courgettes (zucchini) are one vegetable that more skilled gardeners seem to have in abundance, and they're also lovely in cake. The courgette adds moisture to this lemon-flavoured loaf, with a delicate crunch from poppy seeds. The subtle floral perfume of lavender in the glaze offsets the lemon tanginess and lifts the cake straight into summertime.

To make the cake

Preheat the oven to 180°C/160°C fan/350°F/gas 4. Lightly grease and line a 1kg/2lb 4oz (20 x 10cm/8 x 4in) loaf pan.

Leave the skin on the courgette and grate it coarsely. In a clean tea towel, squeeze the moisture from the courgette and set aside.

In a large bowl, beat the butter and sugar with an electric mixer for a few minutes until light and fluffy. Add the eggs, one at a time, and beating each one in well. Beat in the courgette, lemon juice and zest.

Sift in the flour and add the poppy seeds. Mix gently to combine.

Pour into the prepared pan, level to the edges and bake in the oven for 40 minutes, or until a skewer inserted in the centre comes out clean.

Leave to cool for 10 minutes in the pan, then turn out onto a wire rack to cool completely.

To make the lavender glaze

Gently heat the lemon juice in a small saucepan. Remove it from the heat, add the lavender and allow to infuse for 10 minutes. Over a bowl, strain the lavender out of the lemon juice. Beat the cooled infused lemon juice with the icing sugar until smooth. Drizzle over the completely cooled cake and decorate with lavender and lemon.

Vegetable-Dyed Rainbow Cake with Coconut Funfetti

Serves 12

For the colour purées
—

pink: 50g/1¾oz cooked
   beetroot + 8 raspberries
orange: 100g/3½oz peeled
   carrot, cut into chunks
yellow: 100g/3½oz/heaped
   ⅓ cup sweetcorn kernels
   (fresh or frozen)
green: 100g/3½oz/⅔ cup peas
   (fresh or frozen)

For the first two cake layers
—

200g/7oz/scant 1 cup
   unsalted butter, softened
200g/7oz/scant 1 cup
   granulated sugar
3 large free-range eggs
2 tsp vanilla extract

200g/7oz/scant 1⅔ cup
   self-raising flour
2 tsp baking powder
½ tsp salt
butter or non-stick cooking
   spray, for greasing

For the second two
cake layers
—

200g/7oz/scant 1 cup
   unsalted butter, softened
200g/7oz/scant 1 cup
   granulated sugar
3 large free-range eggs
2 tsp vanilla extract
200g/7oz/scant 1⅔ cup
   self-raising flour
2 tsp baking powder
½ tsp salt
butter or non-stick cooking
   spray, for greasing

This is definitely a party cake! When my young children first saw it, they burst into excited cheers. And, knowing what comes from my kitchen, they had fun guessing which vegetable was in each layer. There's no need to use chemical food dyes when vegetables can give such great colours to a rainbow cake. Using carrots, peas, sweetcorn and beetroot, the vegetable purées bring lovely colours to its vanilla flavour. I've added a vanilla icing and then livened it up with naturally coloured coconut funfetti sprinkles.

To make the colour purées
Make sure that you purée the vegetables until very smooth so there are no bits in the cake or the funfetti.

For the pink, purée the beetroot with the raspberries using a hand blender until smooth. Reserve 1 tsp for the funfetti.

For the orange, boil the carrots until soft, then drain and purée with a hand blender until smooth. Reserve 1 tsp for the funfetti.

For the yellow, boil the sweetcorn until soft, then drain and purée with a hand blender until smooth. Reserve ½ tsp for the funfetti.

For the green, boil the peas until soft, then drain and purée with a hand blender until smooth. Reserve ½ tsp for the funfetti.

Set the colours aside.

For the icing
—

300g/10½oz/1⅓ cups unsalted
   butter, softened
600g/1lb 5oz/4¾ cups icing
   (confectioners') sugar
7 tbsp milk
2 tsp vanilla extract

For the coconut funfetti
—

8 tbsp unsweetened
   desiccated (dried flaked)
   coconut
a few drops of vanilla extract
colours from the cake purée
pink: 1 tsp beetroot purée
orange: 1 tsp carrot purée
yellow: ½ tsp sweetcorn purée,
   ¼ tsp water
green: ½ tsp pea purée,
   ¼ tsp water

To make the cakes
Preheat oven to 180°C/160°C fan/350°F/gas 4. Grease two 20cm/
8in round baking pans with butter or non-stick cooking spray.

You will need to make the cake batter twice, in order to cook two
colours of the cake at a time.

For the first two layers, in a large bowl, beat the butter and sugar
together with an electric mixer. Add the eggs, one at a time, and
beating each one in well, then beat in the vanilla.

Sift in the flour, baking powder, and salt, then mix gently
until combined.

Divide the batter evenly between two bowls. Add the pink
vegetable purée to one bowl and fold in gently until evenly
distributed, taking care not to overmix the batter. Spoon into the
prepared pan and spread out evenly. Add the orange purée to
the mixture in the other bowl and mix in the same way.

Continued

The funfetti won't keep, so use it immediately and eat within a few days.

Bake the two layers for 20–25 minutes, or until a skewer inserted in the middle comes out clean.

Leave the cakes to cool in the pan for 10 minutes, then gently turn out onto a wire rack to cool completely.

Repeat with the second set of cake ingredients to make two more cakes and colouring them with the yellow and green purées.

To make the icing
In a large bowl, beat the butter with an electric mixer until smooth, then add the icing sugar, milk and vanilla, and beat until smooth.

Divide the icing into two bowls and save one for the final coat of icing. Using one of the bowls, spread a little icing between each layer, right to the edge, and sandwich together. Spread a little more icing on the very top and sides to create a 'crumb coat' icing layer. It won't cover it entirely, but will make it smooth and stop the final layer getting messy with cake crumbs. Chill the cake in the fridge for 30 minutes to firm up the crumb coat.

To make the coconut funfetti
Place 2 tablespoons of coconut in each of four small bowls.

For the pink, add the beetroot purée and a few drops of vanilla to one of the bowls of coconut and stir until completely combined.

For the orange, add the carrot purée and a few drops of vanilla to the second bowl of coconut and stir until completely combined.

For the yellow, add the sweetcorn purée, a few drops of vanilla and ¼ tsp cold water to a small cup and mix together, then pour into the third bowl of coconut and stir until completely combined.

For the green, add the pea purée, a few drops of vanilla and ¼ tsp cold water to a small cup and mix together, then pour into a bowl of coconut and stir until completely combined.

To finish
Carefully apply the second bowl of buttercream to create the final layer of icing over the top and sides. Using a palette knife, smooth it completely around the cake. Sprinkle with the coconut funfetti in stripes or other patterns.

Spinach and Strawberry Swiss Roll

Serves 8

For the cake

—

75g/2½oz/⅓ cup caster (superfine) sugar, plus extra for sprinkling
100g/3½oz/3⅓ cups spinach leaves
3 large free-range eggs
½ tsp vanilla extract
75g/2½oz/⅔ cup self-raising flour
1 pinch of salt

For the filling

—

120ml/4fl oz/½ cup double (heavy) cream
2 tsp icing (confectioners') sugar
100g/3½oz/1 cup fresh strawberries, hulled and cut into small pieces.

To serve

—

1 tbsp icing (confectioners') sugar

I first encountered spinach and strawberries together in a salad and loved the pairing so much that I was inspired to combine them again in this colourful Swiss roll. The spinach flavour fades away and the vanilla-laced sponge is light and springy – perfect for rolling up with refreshing strawberries and cream.

This Swiss roll is my older sister's favourite of all my veggie desserts. I made it for her years ago and she's mentioned it regularly ever since. Unfortunately, after first making it, I promptly lost the recipe. Now, years later, I knew that it just *had* to be in my book, so I set about recreating it exactly. After a few trials, I hit upon an exact replica of that memorable original. Siobhan, my darling big sister, this one's for you. (Sorry for 'borrowing' your clothes so often when we were teens!)

To make the cake

Preheat the oven to 190°C/170°C fan/375°F/gas 5. Line a 23 x 30cm/9 x 12in Swiss (jelly) roll pan or shallow baking pan, with baking parchment and sprinkle with 1 teaspoon of caster sugar.

Steam the spinach over a pan of boiling water for a minute or so until wilted, then briefly rinse under cold water, drain and squeeze out any excess moisture. Purée with a hand blender until smooth, then set aside.

In a large bowl, beat the eggs, sugar and vanilla with an electric mixer for about 5–10 minutes until very light and fluffy. Add the puréed spinach and beat again until just combined. Sift in the flour and salt, then very gently fold it in, taking care not to overmix.

Pour the batter into the prepared pan, carefully spread to the edges, then bake in the oven for 10 minutes, or until the sides begin to shrink from the edges.

To fill and assemble

While the cake is cooking, lightly dampen a clean tea towel, lay it out on the countertop and sprinkle it with 1 teaspoon of caster sugar.

Continued

When the sponge has finished cooking, immediately turn it out onto the tea towel and carefully remove the baking parchment. Roll the sponge up along the longest side with the tea towel, tightly but gently. Unroll it carefully and allow it to cool completely on the tea towel. This will make it easier to roll with the filling when it's cool.

While the cake is cooling, whip the cream and icing sugar together until thick, then store in the fridge until ready to use.

When the sponge is completely cool, spread it with the whipped cream, leaving a small border around the edges, then sprinkle with the strawberries. Using the tea towel to help, very carefully roll the sponge up along the longest side. Try to keep it tight, but without splitting the sponge or squeezing out the filling. Sift the icing sugar over the roll, then slice into rounds to serve.

Cucumber and Lemon Cake with Gin Icing

Serves 10

For the cake
—

200g/7oz cucumber (about ½ cucumber), washed
½ lemon
150g/5¼oz/⅔ cup unsalted butter, softened, plus extra for greasing
150g/5¼oz/¾ cup granulated sugar
2 large free-range eggs
1½ tsp vanilla extract
250g/9oz/2 cups plain (all-purpose) flour
2 tsp baking powder
½ tsp salt

For the gin icing
—

75g/2½oz/⅓ cup unsalted butter, softened
200g/7oz/1⅔ cups icing (confectioners') sugar
1 tbsp gin or lemon juice

Cucumber and lemon are refreshing in mineral water, but I like them even better in a gin and tonic, so I've taken those flavours and put them together in this delicate pale-green cake. The cucumber comes through subtly, pairing well with the zinginess of the lemon. The gin in the icing adds a botanical note – so be sure to choose your favourite gin for this. For children, or anyone who isn't a fan of gin, just replace it with lemon juice. This is a great cake for a summer party, served with ice-cold G&Ts, of course.

Tip
—

Leave the skin on the cucumber to get the green colour, but do deseed it (see method), otherwise the batter will be too wet. Double the quantities for the icing if you want to completely cover the top and the side of the cake.

To make the cake

Preheat the oven to 170°C/150°C fan/325°F/gas 3. Lightly grease two 18cm/7in round cake pans.

Deseed the cucumber (cut in half lengthways and scrape the seeds out with a teaspoon). Reserve a few slices for decoration, then cut into chunks. Zest and juice the lemon. Purée the cucumber with a hand blender until smooth, then add the lemon zest and juice and mix well.

In a large bowl, cream the butter and sugar with an electric mixer for a few minutes until light and fluffy. Add the eggs, one at a time, and beating each one in well, then beat in the vanilla.

In a separate bowl, sift the flour, baking powder and salt together. Stir one-third of the flour mixture into the egg mixture, then gently mix in one-third of the cucumber. Repeat until everything is combined.

Divide the mixture between the pans. Bake for 25 minutes, or until a skewer inserted in the middle comes out clean. Leave to cool in the pans for 5 minutes, then turn out onto a wire rack to cool completely.

To make the gin icing

In a large bowl, beat the butter, icing sugar and gin together with an electric mixer until smooth and fluffy. Add more icing sugar or gin, if necessary, to reach the consistency of thick frosting. Keep in the fridge until ready to ice the cake.

Sandwich the two layers with half the icing, then spread the remainder over the top. Decorate with the reserved cucumber slices.

Cupcakes

Asparagus and Lemon Cupcakes with Lemon Icing

Makes 12

For the cakes
—

100g/3½oz asparagus,
  woody ends removed
150g/5¼oz/⅔ cup unsalted
  butter, softened
125g/4½oz/⅔ cup granulated
  sugar
2 large free-range eggs
2 tsp vanilla extract
½ tsp lemon juice
½ tsp lemon zest

200g/7oz/1⅔ cups plain
  (all-purpose) flour
2 tsp baking powder
½ tsp salt

For the lemon icing
—

75g/2½oz/⅓ cup unsalted
  butter, softened
150g/5¼oz/1⅛ cup
  icing (confectioners')
  sugar, sifted
1 tsp lemon juice
¼ tsp lemon zest

While I admit that asparagus isn't the most obvious vegetable to put into cupcakes, it has such a lovely spring-like flavour and pairs so beautifully with lemon, that I urge you to try it. Asparagus is lovely griddled with olive oil and lemon, so I've simply taken that a step further (okay, a HUGE step further). A spoonful of puréed asparagus in this lemon batter brings a pretty pale green colour to the sponge, along with a subtle flavour that complements the citrus icing.

Tip
—

A hand blender is the easiest way to purée cooked asparagus. It takes only a few minutes, but be sure to scrape down the sides and purée it until it's smooth so there aren't any pieces in the cupcakes.

To make the cakes
Preheat the oven to 170°C/150°C fan/325°F/gas 3. Line a 12-cup muffin pan with paper cases.

Steam the asparagus for a few minutes until just soft. Drain well and purée until smooth with a hand blender.

In a large bowl, cream together the butter and sugar with an electric mixer. Beat in the eggs, one at a time, and beating each one in well, then beat in the vanilla. Stir in the asparagus purée, lemon juice and zest.

Sift in the flour, baking powder and salt, and fold in gently to combine.

Fill the muffin cups three-quarters full with the batter and bake for 15–20 minutes, or until a skewer inserted in the middle comes out clean.

Leave to cool in the pan for 10 minutes, then turn out onto a wire rack to cool completely.

To make the lemon icing
In a large bowl, beat all the icing ingredients together with an electric mixer until thick. If necessary, add more icing sugar or a teaspoon of milk to reach the desired consistency. Spoon into a piping bag and pipe over the cooled cupcakes.

Chocolate Mashed Potato Cupcakes with Espresso Icing

Makes 12

For the cakes
—

125g/4½oz/½ cup unsalted
   butter, softened
125g/4½oz/⅔ cup
   granulated sugar
2 large free-range eggs
100g/3½oz/½ cup mashed
   potato, cooled (no milk
   or seasoning added)
2 tsp vanilla extract
150g/5¼oz/1¼ cups plain
   (all-purpose) flour

50g/1¾oz/½ cup
   unsweetened cocoa powder
1½ tsp baking powder
½ tsp salt
100ml/3½fl oz/scant
   ½ cup milk

For the espresso icing
—

1 tsp instant coffee granules
3 tbsp milk
75g/2½oz/⅓ cup unsalted
   butter, softened
250g/9oz/2 cups icing
   (confectioners') sugar

Although it sounds unusual, potato has been used in cake for decades. It adds bulk and moisture, plus helps the cake to keep for longer without drying out by giving it an extra richness. It's also a great way to use up leftover mash. Potatoes were plentiful during World War II rationing, so canny bakers used them in cakes to replace some of the fat and sugar that were in short supply. Flipping through my tattered old copy of a cookery book from 1901, I also discovered that a popular dessert even before that was potato pudding, a frankly dull-sounding concoction involving a baked mixture of mashed potato, eggs and lemon juice. I'll stick to cake. These rich, chocolatey cupcakes are topped with espresso-infused icing – essentially a mochaccino in a cupcake!

To make the cakes

Preheat the oven to 170°C/150°C fan/325°F/gas 3. Line a 12-cup muffin pan with paper cases.

In a large bowl, cream the butter and sugar together with an electric mixer until light and fluffy. Add the eggs, one at a time, and beating each one in well. Mix in the mashed potato and vanilla.

In a separate bowl, whisk the flour, cocoa, baking powder and salt. Add a third of the flour to the egg mixture and gently combine, then a third of the milk. Repeat until all the ingredients are combined.

Fill the muffin cups three-quarters full and bake for 15–20 minutes, or until a skewer inserted in the middle comes out clean.

Leave to cool in the pan for 15 minutes, then turn out onto a wire rack to cool completely.

To make the espresso icing

Gently heat the milk and coffee granules in a pan over a medium heat until the coffee dissolves. Leave to cool completely.

In a large bowl, beat the butter with an electric mixer until smooth, then beat in the icing sugar until combined. Beat in the coffee milk slowly until you reach a thick frosting consistency – you may not need all of it. Store in the fridge until ready to use. If the icing is too thick, add a teaspoon of milk to loosen. Spoon the icing into a piping bag and pipe onto the completely cooled cupcakes.

Avocado Chocolate Cupcakes with Cherry Icing

Makes 12

For the cakes
—

1 ripe avocado, peeled
    and pitted
3 tbsp unsalted butter,
    softened
100g/3½oz/½ cup
    granulated sugar
2 large free-range eggs
1 tsp vanilla extract
115g/4oz/generous ¾ cup plus
    1 tbsp plain (all-purpose) flour
30g/1oz/¼ cup unsweetened
    cocoa powder

1½ tsp baking powder
½ tsp salt

For the cherry icing
—

5 cherries, pitted
75g/2½oz/⅓ cup unsalted
    butter, softened
150g/5¼oz/scant 1¼ cups
    icing (confectioners') sugar
2–3 tsp milk (if necessary)

To decorate
—

12 cherries

I know – avocado is a fruit. So, what's it doing in a vegetable desserts book? Well, since, like the tomato, it's mostly used in savoury dishes, I think it's earned its place here. Avocado makes a wonderful replacement for butter in cakes, cookies and other desserts, reducing the calories somewhat and adding extra nutrients. I've topped these rich and fudgy cupcakes with a fresh cherry icing, in homage to that 1970s classic, Black Forest Gâteau.

To make the cakes
Preheat the oven to 170°C/150°C fan/325°F/gas 3. Line a 12-cup muffin pan with paper cases.

In a large bowl, beat the avocado flesh with an electric mixer for a few minutes until creamy. Add the butter and sugar and beat again until light and fluffy. Beat in the eggs, one at a time, and beating each one in well, then beat in the vanilla.

Sift in the flour, cocoa powder, baking powder and salt, and stir gently to combine.

Fill the muffin cups three-quarters full and bake for 15–20 minutes, or until a skewer inserted in the middle comes out clean. Leave to cool in the pans for 10 minutes, then turn out onto a wire rack to cool completely.

To make the cherry icing
Pulverize the cherries with a pestle and mortar until well smashed. Place them into a sieve (strainer) over a bowl and press to extract the juice. You should have at least 1 tablespoon of cherry juice.

In a large bowl, cream the butter with an electric mixer until fluffy. Add the cherry juice and beat until smooth. Sift in the icing sugar, then beat until thick. Add the milk, 1 teaspoon at a time, to make a thick frosting consistency. Spoon the icing into a piping bag and pipe over the cupcakes as desired, topping each one with a cherry.

Parsnip Cupcakes with Chinese Five-Spice Icing

Makes 12

For the cakes
—

100g/3½oz parsnip (1 medium parsnip), peeled
150g/5¼oz/⅔ cup unsalted butter, softened
150g/5¼oz/¾ cup granulated sugar
2 large free-range eggs
2 tsp vanilla extract
200g/7oz/scant 1⅔ cups plain (all-purpose) flour
2 tsp baking powder
½ tsp salt

For the Chinese five-spice icing
—

75g/2½oz/⅓ cup unsalted butter, softened
250g/9oz/2 cups icing (confectioners') sugar
¼ tsp Chinese five-spice powder
2–3 tbsp milk

Like carrot, parsnip works very well in cakes, adding moisture and a subtle earthy sweetness to the sponge. The two behave so similarly in baking that it's surprising carrot cake has been the only veg cake in the spotlight for so long. Perhaps it's finally parsnip's time to shine!

I've used Chinese five-spice in this icing, and although it's traditionally used for savoury dishes, I love the flavours that it brings to desserts, with faint aromas of star anise, Szechuan peppercorns, fennel, cassia and cloves adding a wonderfully complex depth that teases your taste buds with every bite. The elegant piquancy of the icing elevates these cupcakes into something sophisticated.

To make the cakes
Preheat the oven to 170°C/150°C fan/325°F/gas 3. Line a 12-cup muffin pan with paper cases.

Finely grate the parsnip with a grater or in a food processor. Set aside.

In a large bowl, cream together the butter and sugar with an electric mixer until fluffy. Beat in the eggs, one at a time, and beating each one in well, then beat in the parsnip and vanilla.

Sift in the flour, baking powder and salt, and stir gently to combine.

Fill the muffin cups three-quarters full and bake for 15–20 minutes, or until a skewer inserted in the middle comes out clean.

Leave to cool in the pan for 10 minutes, then turn out onto a wire rack to cool completely.

To make the Chinese five-spice icing
In a large bowl, cream the butter with an electric mixer until smooth. Sift in the icing sugar and five-spice powder and beat until thick. Beat in the milk, a tablespoon at a time, only using if necessary to make it a frosting consistency.

Spoon the icing into a piping bag and pipe onto the completely cooled cupcakes.

Spinach and Coconut Cupcakes with Coconut Icing

Makes 18

For the cakes
—

150g/5¼oz/5 cups spinach
125g/4½oz/⅔ cup
  unsalted butter, softened
125g/4½oz/⅔ cup
  granulated sugar
2 large free-range eggs
100 ml/3½fl oz/scant ½ cup
  full-fat coconut milk
2 tsp vanilla extract
150g/5¼oz/1¼ cup plain
  (all-purpose) flour
1½ tsp baking powder

½ tsp salt
75g/2½oz/¾ cup desiccated
  (dried flaked) coconut

For the coconut icing
—

50g/1¾oz/¼ cup unsalted
  butter, softened
200g/7oz/1⅔ cups icing
  (confectioners') sugar
2 tbsp full-fat coconut milk

To serve
—

3 tbsp desiccated
  (dried flaked) coconut

Spinach and coconut work very well together in savoury dishes like curry, soup, American-style creamed spinach and the popular spiced Caribbean side-dish callaloo. They also pair well in smoothies, and it was not the first time a breakfast recipe has inspired me to try something new in the cake department! As I blitzed spinach, coconut milk and ice in my blender, I instantly knew that the combination would be perfect for cupcakes. I was right. The spinach brings a vivid green to the sponge that tastes of creamy, tropical coconut.

To make the cakes

Preheat the oven to 170°C/150°C fan/325°F/gas 3. Line a 12-cup muffin pan with paper cases.

Steam or simmer the spinach for a few minutes until wilted. Run under cold water to refresh, drain and squeeze out any excess moisture. Purée well with a hand blender and set aside.

Cream the butter and sugar together with an electric mixer for a few minutes until light and fluffy. Add the eggs, one at a time, and beating each one in well. Mix in the spinach purée, coconut milk and vanilla.Sift in the flour, baking powder and salt, then add the desiccated coconut and mix gently until just combined.

Fill the muffin cups three-quarters full and bake for 15–20 minutes, or until a skewer inserted in the middle comes out clean. Leave to cool in the pan for 15 minutes, then turn out onto a wire rack and leave to cool completely.

To make the coconut icing

In a large bowl, beat the butter with an electric mixer until soft. Beat in the icing sugar and coconut milk until thick and fluffy. If necessary, add a little more coconut milk or icing sugar to reach the desired consistency. Store in the fridge until ready to use.

Spoon the icing into a piping bag and pipe onto the completely cooled cupcakes, then sprinkle with desiccated coconut.

Pumpkin Cupcakes with Avocado Icing

Makes 12

For the cakes
—

125g/4½oz/½ cup unsalted
   butter, softened
125g/4½oz/⅔ cup granulated
   sugar
2 large free-range eggs
150g/5¼oz/½ cup pumpkin
   purée (canned or purée
   cooked pumpkin or
   butternut squash)
2 tsp vanilla extract
175g/6oz/heaped 1⅓ cups
   plain (all-purpose) flour

2 tsp baking powder
1 tsp ground cinnamon
½ tsp ground nutmeg
½ tsp ground ginger
½ tsp ground allspice
½ tsp salt
100ml/3½floz/scant
   ½ cup milk

For the avocado icing
—

1 ripe avocado, pitted
   and peeled
250g/9oz/2 cups icing
   (confectioners') sugar
½ tsp lemon juice

These autumnal spiced cupcakes are almost ghoulish-looking. Pumpkin turns the cupcakes orange, while using avocado instead of butter in the icing introduces a vibrant green. The avocado flavour is softened by the lemon and sugar but it still stays firm enough for piping.

Tip
—

Canned pumpkin purée is available in many major supermarkets, but you can make your own by puréeing cooked butternut or other squash. You could also steam and purée the stringy orange innards of a fresh carved pumpkin at Halloween.

<u>To make the cakes</u>
Preheat the oven to 170°C/150°C fan/325°F/gas 3. Line a 12-cup muffin pan with paper cases.

Cream the butter and sugar together until light and fluffy. Beat in the eggs, one at a time, and beating each one in well, then beat in the pumpkin and vanilla.

Into a separate bowl, sift the flour, baking powder, spices and salt.

Alternating, add one-third of the flour to the egg mixture and stir to combine, then one-third of the milk. Repeat until all the ingredients are combined.

Spoon the batter into the muffin cases until nearly full. Bake for 15–20 minutes, or until a skewer inserted in the middle comes out clean. Leave to cool in the pan for 10 minutes, then turn out onto a wire rack to cool completely before icing.

<u>To make the avocado icing</u>
Purée the avocado with a hand blender until smooth and creamy, then transfer to a large bowl. Add the icing sugar and lemon juice then beat with an electric mixer until thick. You may need to add more icing sugar, depending on the size of your avocado, to get a thick piping consistency. Spoon into a piping bag and frost the completely cooled cupcakes as desired. Store in the refrigerator until ready to use.

Beetroot and Vanilla Cupcakes with Beetroot Icing

Makes 12

For the cakes
—

100g/3½oz cooked beetroot (boiled, steamed, roasted or store-bought vacuum sealed without vinegar)
150g/5¼oz/⅔ cup unsalted butter, softened
125g/4½oz/⅔ cup granulated sugar
2 large free-range eggs
2 tsp vanilla extract

200g/7oz/scant 1⅔ cup plain (all-purpose) flour
2 tsp baking powder
½ tsp salt

For the icing
—

75g/2½oz/⅓ cup unsalted butter, softened
250g/9oz/2 cups icing (confectioners') sugar
1 tbsp milk
1 tsp beetroot juice
½ tsp vanilla extract

Through many tests over the years, I've found that the best way to create beetroot cupcakes that taste delicious, look subtly pink and have a light texture is not to include too much beetroot! Due to pH levels and other technicalities, tinkering with the acidity of the cakes negatively affects both texture and taste. So don't expect vibrant purple cupcakes – just really tasty ones. The pink colour of this vanilla sponge is more vibrant on top and fades to the bottom in a beautiful ombré effect.

Tip
—

If you use vacuum-sealed pre-cooked beetroot, you can easily salvage some juice for the icing. If you cook your own beetroots, just press a little of the beetroot purée through a sieve (fine-mesh strainer) over a bowl to collect a teaspoon of juice.

To make the cakes
Preheat the oven to 170°C/150°C fan/325°F/gas 3. Line a 12-cup muffin pan with paper cases.

Purée the cooked beetroot until smooth.

Cream the butter and sugar together until light and fluffy. Beat in the eggs, one at a time, and beating each one in well, then beat in the beetroot purée and vanilla. Don't worry if the batter splits, it will come together when the flour is added.

Sift in the flour, baking powder and salt, and stir gently to combine.

Spoon the batter into the muffin cases until three-quarters full. Bake for 15–20 minutes, or until a skewer inserted in the middle comes out clean.

Leave to cool in the pan for 10 minutes, then transfer to a wire rack to cool completely before icing.

To make the beetroot icing
In a large bowl, cream the butter with an electric mixer until smooth. Sift in the icing sugar and beat until thick. Beat in the milk, beetroot juice and vanilla. If necessary, add more icing sugar or a teaspoon of milk to reach the consistency of thick frosting.

Spoon the icing into a piping bag and pipe onto the completely cooled cupcakes.

Cavolo Nero and Orange Cupcakes with Orange Icing

Makes 12

For the cakes

—

40g/1¼oz/½ cup cavolo nero leaves, thick stalks discarded
150g/5¼oz/⅔ cup unsalted butter, softened
150g/5¼oz/¾ cup granulated sugar
2 large free-range eggs
2 tsp vanilla extract
2 tbsp orange zest
4 tbsp orange juice
200g/7oz/scant 1⅔ cups plain (all-purpose) flour
1 tsp baking powder
½ tsp salt

For the orange icing

—

75g/2½oz/⅓ cup unsalted butter, softened
250g/9oz/2 cups icing (confectioners') sugar
2–3 tbsp orange juice

Originally from Tuscany, cavolo nero (aka Italian kale or black kale) is a leafy cabbage with really dark green, almost black, leaves. My local farmers' market was piled high with freshly picked leaves, so I decided to try them in some cakes. I start most mornings with a green smoothie, so I've taken my breakfast flavours as the inspiration here and turned them into these intensely coloured cupcakes, which have a delightful taste of orange.

Tip

—

If you can't get cavolo nero, just substitute curly kale, spinach or Swiss chard.

To make the cakes

Preheat the oven to 170°C/150°C fan/325°F/gas 3. Line a 12-cup muffin pan with paper cases.

Chop the cavolo nero leaves into bite-sized pieces and boil or steam for a few minutes until tender. Refresh by rinsing under cold water, then drain and squeeze out any excess moisture. Chop finely. Purée it with a hand blender – it will still be a bit stringy, but you want it to be as smooth a paste as possible to get the best colour. If necessary, add the orange juice to make it easier to purée, then set aside.

In a large bowl, cream the butter and sugar with an electric mixer until light and fluffy. Beat in the eggs, one at a time, and beating each one in well, then beat in the cavolo nero, vanilla, orange juice and zest. The batter may split, but it will come together when the flour is added.

Sift in the flour, baking powder and salt, and stir gently to combine.

Fill the muffin cups three-quarters full with the batter and bake for 20 minutes, or until a skewer inserted in the middle comes out clean. Leave to cool in the pan for 10 minutes, then turn out onto a wire rack and leave to cool completely.

To make the orange icing

In a large bowl, cream the butter with an electric mixer until fluffy, then add the icing sugar and beat until thick. Add enough of the orange juice to make it a frosting consistency – you may not need all of it. Store in the fridge until ready to use.

Spoon the icing into a piping bag and pipe over the cooled cupcakes.

Spiced Butternut Squash Muffins with Walnuts and Crystallized Ginger

Makes 12

125g/4½oz/1 cup plain (all-purpose) flour
100g/3½oz/scant ¾ cup plain wholemeal flour
2 tsp baking powder
2 tsp ground cinnamon
½ tsp salt
150g/5¼oz/1½ cups finely shredded butternut squash (peeled and deseeded)

50g/1¾oz/½ cup walnuts, chopped
50g/1¾oz/½ cup crystallized ginger, finely diced
120ml/4¼fl oz/½ cup vegetable oil
100g/3½oz/scant ½ cup plain Greek yogurt
100g/3½oz/scant ½ cup granulated sugar
3 large free-range eggs
2 tsp vanilla extract

These soft, fluffy, lightly spiced muffins are filled with grated butternut squash. I like having a bit of texture in muffins, so I've added chopped walnuts and some bursts of fiery spice with crystallized ginger. They contain less oil than would typically be in a muffin of this sort, since some is substituted with plain Greek yogurt – a trick that I use often in baking. I've also replaced some of the plain (all-purpose) flour with wholemeal to give the muffins some extra fibre and goodness.

Preheat the oven to 170°C/150°C fan/325°F/gas 3. Grease a 12-cup muffin pan with paper cases.

In a large bowl, sift the flours, baking powder, cinnamon and salt (adding any sieved bran back into the bowl), then stir in the butternut squash, walnuts and ginger.

In a separate bowl, whisk the oil, yogurt, sugar, eggs and vanilla, then pour into the flour mixture. Stir until just combined, then spoon the batter into the muffin cases until nearly full and bake for 15–20 minutes, or until a skewer inserted in the middle comes out clean.

Leave to cool in the pan for a few minutes, then turn out onto a wire rack to cool completely.

Pea and Mint Cupcakes with Rose Water Buttercream

Makes 12

For the cakes
—

100g/3½oz/⅔ cup peas
  (fresh or frozen)
1 tbsp chopped fresh
  mint leaves
115g/4oz/½ cup unsalted
  butter, softened
125g/4½oz/⅔ cup
  granulated sugar
2 large free-range eggs
1 tsp vanilla extract
150g/5¼oz/1¼ cups plain
  (all-purpose) flour

2 tsp baking powder
1 pinch of salt

For the rose water buttercream
—

75g/2½oz/⅓ cup unsalted
  butter, softened
150g/5¼oz/scant 1¼ cups
  icing (confectioners') sugar
¼–½ tsp rose water
1–2 tbsp milk

To decorate
—

12 dried culinary rose buds or
  petals (optional)

The sweet, delicate flavour of garden peas is even more delectable when garnished with fresh, cool mint. I love minted peas mashed on toast in the morning, while fresh pea and mint soup is an absolute joy. Here, I've brought them together into lovely, springy cupcakes that have a subtle hint of mint flavour. Topped with a gently fragrant rose water buttercream, it's like walking through an English cottage garden on a summer morning. Podding peas and sneaking the occasional raw, sweet green orb to eat is one of life's simple pleasures, but frozen peas work equally well and are, admittedly, far more convenient.

To make the cakes
Preheat the oven to 170°C/150°C fan/325°F/gas 3. Line a 12-cup muffin pan with paper cases.

Boil the peas for a few minutes until soft, then rinse under cold water and drain. Purée the peas with the mint with a hand blender until smooth and set aside.

In a large bowl, cream the butter and sugar together with an electric mixer until light and fluffy. Add the eggs, one at a time, and beating each one in well, then beat in the vanilla and pea purée.

Sift in the flour, baking powder and salt, and stir gently to combine.

Spoon the batter into the muffin pan to three-quarters full, then bake for 15–20 minutes, or until a skewer inserted in the middle comes out clean. Leave to cool in the pan for 5 minutes, then turn out onto a wire rack to cool completely.

To make the rose water buttercream
In a large bowl, beat the butter, icing sugar, rose water and 1 tablespoon of milk together with an electric mixer until smooth and fluffy. Add more milk, if necessary, to make a thick frosting consistency. Keep in the fridge until ready to ice the cupcakes.

Spoon the icing into a piping bag and frost the completely cooled cupcakes as desired, then top with dried rose buds, if you like.

Tip
—

Too much rose water can be overpowering, so pour with a steady hand and use sparingly, tasting before adding more.

Cookies

Sweetcorn and White Chocolate Cookies with Blackberry Glaze

Makes 25

For the cookies
—

150g/5¼oz/¾ cup
sweetcorn kernels
(fresh or frozen)
120g/4¼oz/½ cup
unsalted butter, melted
150g/5¼oz/¾ cup
granulated sugar
1 tsp vanilla extract
275g/10oz/2¼ cup plain
(all-purpose) flour
½ tsp baking powder
⅛ tsp salt
100g/3½oz/½ cup white
chocolate, chopped

For the blackberry glaze
—

10 blackberries (fresh or
frozen and thawed)
6 tbsp icing (confectioners')
sugar

Inspired by the flavours of late autumn, these cookies are a contrast of sweet and tangy. The flavour of the sweetcorn comes through very pleasantly and is lovely alongside the creamy rich chunks of white chocolate. The blackberry glaze is vibrant, and at once both sweet and tart, cutting nicely through the baked sweetness of the cookies.

There's a famous recipe for sweetcorn cookies from a New York restaurant, but it calls for freeze-dried corn powder. I don't like recipes that necessitate an online shop or visits to expensive specialist stores to find unusual ingredients, so I've developed my own version using puréed corn, which replaces the egg.

To make the cookies
Preheat the oven to 170°C/150°Cfan/325°F/gas 3. Line two baking sheets with baking parchment.

Boil the sweetcorn for a few minutes until cooked. Rinse under cold water, drain and purée with a hand blender.

In a large bowl, whisk the melted butter and sugar. Whisk in the corn purée and vanilla, then add the flour, baking powder and salt, and combine. Stir in the chocolate.

Roll teaspoons of the mixture into balls, place them onto the prepared baking sheets, and flatten them slightly with your fingertips or the heel of your hand. Bake for 12 minutes, or until just beginning to turn golden.

Transfer to a wire rack and leave to cool completely.

To make the blackberry glaze
Place the blackberries into a sieve (strainer) over a bowl and press with a spoon to extract the juice (about 1 tablespoon). Stir the icing sugar into the blackberry juice and mix until smooth. Add a little water or more sugar if necessary to reach a thick drizzling consistency. Drizzle over the completely cooled cookies.

Parsnip Tuile Baskets with Strawberries and Cream

Makes 10

For the baskets
—

25g/1oz parsnip (½ small
  parsnip), peeled
1 egg white
50g/1¾oz/¼ cup caster
  (superfine) sugar
30g/1oz/⅛ cup unsalted
  butter, melted and cooled
30g/1oz/¼ cup plain
  (all-purpose) flour

For the filling
—

100ml/3½fl oz/
  scant ½ cup double
  (heavy) cream
1 large handful of
  strawberries
10 sprigs of mint

These parsnip tuile baskets take just minutes to make and are delicate, light, sweet and crisp – perfect for filling with seasonal fruit. They will soften quickly, so serve them immediately if you want them crisp and brittle.

Tip
—

You can adapt these little baskets to whichever berries or filling you have to hand, but I love the freshness of the cream with sweet seasonal strawberries. They also work well as little edible bowls for chocolate mousse or ice cream.

To make the baskets
Preheat the oven to 200°C/180°C fan/400°F/gas 6 and line two baking sheets with parchment paper. Grease the underside of a muffin pan (for forming the baskets).

Very finely grate the raw parsnip in a mini food processor or with the small holes of a manual grater.

In a large bowl, beat the egg white and sugar with an electric mixer until frothy, then gently stir in the parsnip, butter and flour.

Spoon a tablespoon of the mixture onto the prepared baking sheet and spread into a large round with the back of a spoon as thinly as possible to about 13cm/5in diameter. Repeat to make 10. Cook for 5–7 minutes until the edges begin to brown.

To prepare the filling
Meanwhile, beat the cream and sugar until thick, then store in the fridge until ready to use. Cut the strawberries in half or quarters depending on their size.

To shape the baskets
When the tuiles have finished cooking, use a spatula to carefully remove them immediately from the parchment and place them over the upturned muffin cups, gently pressing to form them into basket shapes. Leave to cool completely over the upturned muffin cups for about a minute.

Spoon the cream into the baskets, then top with the strawberries and a sprig of mint. Serve immediately.

Sweet Potato and Salted Hazelnut Cookies

Makes 18

115g/4oz/½ cup unsalted
  butter, melted and cooled
100g/3½oz/½ cup light
  soft brown sugar
50g/1¾oz/¼ cup
  granulated sugar
125g/4½oz/½ cup mashed
  cooked sweet potato
  (steamed or roasted)

1 tsp vanilla extract
225g/8oz/2 cups plain
  (all-purpose) flour
½ tsp bicarbonate of soda
  (baking soda)
¼ tsp salt
75g/2½oz/½ cup salted
  hazelnuts

These soft, chewy cookies envelop little treasure troves of salted hazelnuts, bringing a contrasting flavour and crunch. But there's more to them than that. Their other clever secret is that the sweet potato not only brings bulk, texture and sweetness, but it also replaces the egg in the recipe. Thanks mash, that'll be more eggs saved for breakfast, then!

Tip
—

Be sure not to overbake these cookies. If you want that chewy texture that comes when they slightly collapse as they begin to cool, don't wait for them to turn too golden.

Preheat the oven to 180°C/160°C fan/350°F/gas 4. Line two baking sheets with baking parchment.

In a large bowl, whisk the melted butter and sugars together well, then whisk in the vanilla and mashed sweet potato. Add the flour, bicarbonate of soda and salt, and stir to create a dough, then stir in the hazelnuts.

Roll heaped tablespoons of the dough into balls, place them onto the prepared baking sheet and press down gently with the heel of your hand. Bake for 10 minutes. They will be pale, but don't overbake them.

Leave to cool for a few minutes on the baking sheets, then transfer to a wire rack to cool completely.

Carrot, Mango and Oat Cookies

Makes 15–20

50g/1¾oz/¼ cup unsalted butter, softened
75g/2½oz/⅓ cup light soft brown sugar
1 large free-range egg
1 tsp vanilla extract
1 mango, peeled and diced

100g/3½oz carrot (1 medium carrot), peeled and grated
100g/3½oz/⅔ cup rolled oats
150g/5¼oz/1¼ cup plain wholemeal flour
½ tsp baking powder
½ tsp ground cinnamon
¼ tsp ground ginger
¼ tsp salt

The sweet perfume and succulent texture of mango is perfect alongside the fresh, sweet taste of carrots in these chewy and delicately spiced oat cookies. I love how the mild flavour of carrots makes them so versatile. Plus they're wonderful for adding texture and a little extra nutrition to so many dishes. Aside from the usual salads, I like to grate carrots into porridge with ground cinnamon in the morning, or onto yogurt with some maple syrup. I often use them in cookies, either whizzing until fine before incorporating into a sugar cookie dough or, as I've done here, mixing into hearty oat cookies.

Preheat the oven to 170°C/150°C fan/325°F/gas 3. Line a baking sheet with baking parchment.

In a large bowl, mix together the butter and sugar until well combined. Add the egg and vanilla and mix well, then stir in the mango and carrot. Mix in the oats, flour, baking powder, spices and salt.

With damp hands, roll tablespoonfuls of the mixture into balls, place onto the prepared baking sheet and flatten slightly with a fork.

Bake for 15 minutes, or until lightly golden.

Leave to cool on the baking sheet for 5 minutes, then transfer to a wire rack to cool completely.

Pumpkin Gingernuts

Makes 30–40

125g/4½oz/½ cup
  unsalted butter
75g/2½oz/¼ cup golden
  (corn) syrup
350g/12oz/scant 3 cups
  self-raising flour

150g/5¼oz/¾ cup caster
  (superfine) sugar
1 tbsp ground ginger
2–3 tsp bicarbonate of soda
  (baking soda)
100g/3½oz/½ cup pumpkin
  purée (canned, or cooked
  and puréed fresh pumpkin
  or butternut squash)

The smell of homemade gingernuts baking is absolutely magical, sending their heady scents of pure autumn wafting around the kitchen, conjuring images of a breeze of crisp fallen leaves and snuggly scarves. Pumpkin is undoubtedly the foodstuff of the season, so I've used it to replace the egg in these cookies and to enhance their structure. It's pretty much mandatory that you'll need to eat these with a cup of hot tea.

Tip
—

This recipe makes crispy cookies, but if you prefer them softer, then don't flatten them quite so much and cook them for just 15–20 minutes. They'll then be chewier in the middle.

Preheat the oven to 160°C/140°C fan/320°F/gas 2. Line two baking sheets with baking parchment.

Melt the butter and syrup together in a pan over a medium heat, then remove from the heat and leave to cool slightly.

Sift the flour, sugar, ginger and bicarbonate of soda into a large bowl.

Stir the pumpkin into the melted butter/syrup mixture and mix well, then pour it into the bowl of dry ingredients. Stir to combine well.

Roll teaspoons of the mixture into balls, place them on the prepared baking sheets and flatten them slightly with your fingertips or the heel of your hand to about 5mm/¼in thick. Bake for 20–25 minutes, or until golden.

Transfer to a wire rack and leave to cool completely.

Swede, Nutmeg Cookies with Maple-Candied Seeds

Makes 30

225g/8oz/1 cup unsalted
  butter, softened
125g/4½oz/⅔ cup
  granulated sugar
1 large free-range egg
1 tsp vanilla extract
50g/1¾oz/¾ cup swede
  (rutabaga), peeled and
  finely grated
275g/10oz/2½ cups plain
  (all-purpose) flour

½ tsp freshly grated nutmeg
¼ tsp bicarbonate of soda
  (baking soda)
¼ tsp salt

For the
maple-candied seeds
—

100g/3½oz/¾ cup
  mixed seeds
6 tbsp maple syrup
½ tsp vanilla extract
¼ tsp salt

The swede (rutabaga) in these crisp cookies adds bulk and a sweet, earthy flavour that pairs well with the fragrant nutmeg and shows in little golden flecks through the mixture. I think the humble swede (rutabaga) deserves a bit of love, so I've topped these cookies with a glossy crown of maple-candied mixed seeds – like sweet glistening jewels – to add more crunch and a sweet maple flavour. The seeds will get very hot, so use spoons and work quickly to pile them onto the warm cookies as they'll adhere as they cool.

To make the cakes

In a large bowl, beat the butter and sugar with an electric mixer until fluffy. Add the egg and vanilla and beat again. Mix in the grated swede. Add the flour, nutmeg, bicarbonate of soda and salt, and stir to combine. It is a stiff mixture so you may need to use your hands to bring it together. Wrap the dough in cling film (plastic wrap) and refrigerate for at least an hour or overnight.

Preheat the oven to 180°C/160°C fan/350°F/gas 4. Line two baking sheets with baking parchment.

Roll heaped teaspoons of the dough into balls and place onto the prepared baking sheets, flattening slightly with the heel of your hand. Bake for 12 minutes, or until they just begin to turn golden.

Leave to cool for a few minutes on the baking sheet, then transfer to a wire rack to cool completely.

To make the maple-candied seeds

Heat a dry non-stick frying pan over a medium heat until hot. Add the seeds, maple syrup, vanilla and salt, and stir often for 2–3 minutes until the seeds are coated and the mixture is thick and reduced. Be careful – the mixture will be very hot.

When the cookies come out of the oven, use two spoons to heap a small amount of the candied seeds onto each one, then leave to cool.

Spinach and Almond Shortbread

Makes 10–20

100g/3½oz/3⅓ cups
  spinach leaves
125g/4½oz/½ cup unsalted
  butter, softened

50g/1¾oz/¼ cup caster
  (superfine) sugar,
  plus extra to finish
½ tsp almond extract
225g/8oz/1¾ cup plain
  (all-purpose) flour,
  plus extra for dusting

I love the bright green colour of these rich and buttery shortbread cookies, which have a gentle flavour from the almond extract. My mum made shortbread, though it was never green! It's so easy to make that it's obvious why it holds nostalgic memories for so many. I remember helping to roll and prick the shortbread with a fork, ready to bake for imminent guests.

Tip

—

Be sure to purée the spinach completely to a paste in order to get the brightest, most uniformly green colour. You can cut the shortbread into triangles or rectangles, or use cookie cutters to make other shapes.

Preheat the oven to 180°C/160°C fan/350°F/gas 4. Line a baking sheet with baking parchment.

Wilt the spinach in a pan with a small amount of boiling water, then drain and run under cold water to refresh. Squeeze out the moisture. Purée the spinach with a hand blender until smooth.

In a large bowl, beat the butter and sugar together with an electric mixer until smooth and fluffy. Add the spinach purée and almond extract and beat well. Sift in the flour and mix. Turn the mixture onto a lightly floured surface and knead for a few minutes until it forms a soft dough.

Place the dough between two pieces of baking parchment and roll it out to 1cm/½in thick. Cut into desired shapes (rectangles, triangles or with cookie cutters) and place onto the prepared baking sheet, using your finger to gently smooth any edges that look ragged from the spinach. Lightly prick the shortbread with a fork. Re-roll and repeat with any off-cuts of dough. Chill the shortbread for 30 minutes in the fridge.

Lightly sprinkle the shortbread with a little caster sugar, then bake for 15–20 minutes, or until the edges begin to turn slightly golden.

Leave to cool for 5 minutes on the baking sheet, then transfer to a wire rack to cool completely.

Parsnip Coconut Macaroons

Makes 12

2 large free-range
  egg whites
½ tsp cornflour (cornstarch)
100g/3½oz/½ cup caster
  (superfine) sugar
200g/7oz/3 cups
  unsweetened desiccated
  (dried flaked) coconut
50g/1¾oz/⅔ cup parsnip
  (½ medium parsnip), peeled
  and grated

25g/⅘oz/¼ cup ground
  almonds
1 tsp vanilla extract
⅛ tsp salt

To finish
—
75g/2½oz good-quality dark
  chocolate (optional)

These coconut macaroons are so quick and easy to make, requiring just a bit of grating, egg white whipping and waiting. They are baked until just golden and then allowed to cool before being drizzled with oozy melted chocolate. They're very delicate when they come out of the oven, so slide a palette knife carefully underneath to remove them from the parchment. They'll firm up when they cool on a wire rack.

Preheat the oven to 170°C/150°C fan/325°F/gas 3. Line a baking sheet with baking parchment.

Whisk the egg whites with an electric mixer until they become frothy. Add the cornflour and continue whisking until soft peaks form. Continue whisking and add the sugar a tablespoon at a time until the egg whites form stiff peaks. Gently fold in the coconut, parsnip, ground almonds, vanilla and salt.

Drop tablespoonfuls of the mixture in small heaps slightly apart on the prepared baking sheets, then bake for 15 minutes, or until the macaroons turn golden. Gently remove from the baking parchment (you may need to slide a palette knife under them), then transfer to a wire rack to cool completely.

Meanwhile, melt the chocolate in a microwave or double boiler (in a bowl over a pan of simmering water, but don't let the bottom of the bowl touch the water). When the macaroons have cooled, drizzle them with the melted chocolate.

Kale Chocolate Cookies

Makes 30

75g/2½oz/2 packed cups
  kale leaves, thick stems
  discarded
120g/4¼oz/scant ⅔ cup
  unsalted butter, softened
75g/2½oz/scant ½ cup light
  soft brown sugar
75g/2½oz/scant ⅓ cup
  granulated sugar
1 large free-range egg, beaten
1 tsp vanilla extract
140g/5oz/scant 1¼ cups
  plain (all-purpose) flour
3 tbsp unsweetened cocoa
  powder
½ tsp bicarbonate of soda
  (baking soda)
⅛ tsp salt
200g/7oz good-quality
  dark chocolate, chopped

Chewy and rich, these double chocolate cookies are delightfully indulgent. I dare you not to try one warm from the oven, with the chocolate melting with every bite. Flecks of green kale are nestled amongst the chocolate chunks, the only quiet evidence of the goodness of leafy greens in these cookies.

Tip
—

Be sure to chop the kale very finely for the best texture.

Preheat the oven to 170°C/150°C fan/ 325°F/gas 3. Line two baking sheets with baking parchment.

Chop the kale into bite-sized pieces, then steam for a few minutes until soft. Rinse under cold water, drain and then chop very finely or whiz in a food processor.

In a large bowl, cream the butter and sugar with an electric mixer until light, then beat in the eggs, vanilla and kale.

Sift the flour, cocoa powder and baking powder into the wet mixture and gently stir to combine. Add the chopped chocolate and mix.

Drop teaspoonfuls of the mixture onto the prepared baking sheets, spaced slightly apart, then bake for 10–12 minutes until the edges are set but the middles still soft. Take care not to overbake.

Leave the cookies to cool for a few minutes on the baking sheets, then transfer to a wire rack to cool completely.

Romanesco, Lemon and Cardamom Cookies

Makes 15–20

150g/5½oz/¾ cup
   romanesco (or cauliflower)
100g/3½oz/scant ½ cup
   unsalted butter, softened
100g/3½oz/scant ½ cup
   granulated sugar
zest and juice of 1 lemon
100g/3½oz/⅔ cup rolled oats
125g/4½oz/1 cup
   self-raising flour
8 cardamom pods
¼ tsp salt

I'm always intrigued by romanesco, which looks like a spiky cross between a broccoli and a cauliflower. Although it's rare to spot one on a supermarket shelf, farmers' markets are piled high from late summer to early autumn with the psychedelic-looking brassicas.

Those bizarre, yellow-green spirals taste like cauliflower and can be cooked in the same way, steamed, boiled or baked. Here, I've added romanesco to lemon cardamom cookies, which showcase its mild, sweetly nutty taste. The cardamom brings a warm, spicy aroma to the cookies against the citrus backdrop.

Tip
—

You can bake the cookies with cauliflower, too, when romanesco is out of season.

Preheat the oven to 180°C/160°C fan/350°F/gas 4. Line a baking sheet with baking parchment.

Finely grate the romanesco or whiz it in a food processor until it resembles fine crumbs. Set aside.

Cream the butter and sugar with an electric whisk until light and fluffy. Add the lemon zest and juice and mix well.

In a pestle and mortar, crush the cardamom pods to release the seeds and discard the empty pods. Bash the seeds for a minute or so until lightly ground.

Stir the romanesco, oats, flour, ground cardamom and salt into the batter and stir gently to combine.

With damp hands, roll tablespoonfuls of the batter into balls, place on the prepared baking sheet and press down lightly with a fork. Bake for 15 minutes, or until lightly golden.

Leave to cool on the baking sheet for 5 minutes, then transfer to a wire rack to cool completely.

Squares
+
Traybakes

Sweet Potato and Pecan Blondies

Makes 16

115g/4oz/½ cup unsalted butter, melted, plus extra for greasing
150g/5¼oz/¾ cup packed light soft brown sugar
125g/4½oz/generous ½ cup mashed cooked sweet potato (steamed or roasted)

1 tsp vanilla extract
125g/4½oz/1 cup plain (all-purpose) flour
½ tsp baking powder
¼ tsp salt
100g/3½oz milk chocolate, chopped
50g/1¾oz/½ cup pecans, roughly chopped

Don't be tempted to cut into these brownies before they're completely cooled or you'll end up with a squidgy mess. Patience is key here. Try to ignore the smell of the caramelized brown sugar, the melting chocolate and hot pecan. If you have the willpower to wait until they're cold, you'll be rewarded with decadent sweet potato blondie squares that have that characteristic chewy texture, with a gooey soft centre and nice crispy edges. That said, I'd happily add a scoop of vanilla ice cream to these blondies while they're still warm and pass around spoons to tuck in. Because sometimes patience has no place when a squidgy mess is this delicious.

For this recipe, the sweet potato replaces the egg, giving the bake structure, moisture and a lovely orange colour. Thanks, sweet potatoes!

Preheat the oven to 180°C/160°C fan/350°F/gas 4. Lightly grease a 20cm/8in square baking pan.

In a large bowl, whisk the melted butter and sugar together. Whisk in the mashed sweet potato and vanilla, then sift in the flour, baking powder and salt, and mix well. Add the chocolate and pecans and stir to combine.

Spoon the batter into the prepared baking pan and spread to the edges evenly. Bake for 20 minutes, or until the edges are firm and the middle is just set. It will look slightly underdone in the middle but will continue cooking as it cools.

Leave to cool completely in the baking pan before cutting into squares.

Spinach and Lemon Bars

Makes 16

For the base
—

75g/2½oz/2½ cups
  spinach leaves
75g/2½oz/⅓ cup unsalted
  butter, softened, plus extra
  for greasing
2 tbsp caster (superfine)
  sugar, plus extra to finish
115g/4oz/scant 1 cup plain
  (all-purpose) flour

For the lemon filling
—

4 large free-range eggs
200g/7oz/scant 1 cup
  granulated sugar
150ml/5fl oz/⅔ cup lemon
  juice (from about 4 lemons)
3 tbsp lemon zest
40g/1¼oz/⅓ cup plain
  (all-purpose) flour
1 tbsp butter

To finish
—

1 tbsp icing (confectioners')
  sugar

Spinach? Why not? If ever there's an opportunity to add some leafy greens to a dessert, I'll take it — it must surely add a little goodness to counteract some of the sugar. The spinach makes the base a lovely natural green colour, which provides a striking contrast to the bright yellow lemon curd — smooth, creamy and melting against the firm buttery shortbread.

Preheat the oven to 180°C/160°C fan/350°F/gas 4. Grease and line a 20cm/8in square baking pan.

Wilt the spinach in a pan with a small amount of boiling water, then run under cold water to refresh, then squeeze out the moisture. Purée with a hand blender until smooth.

In a large bowl, beat the butter and sugar together with an electric mixer until smooth, but not too fluffy and aerated. Add the spinach purée and beat well. Sift in the flour and mix gently.

Pour the mixture into the prepared pan, spread to the edges and press down firmly with the back of a damp spoon. Be sure that the mixture goes right into all the edges and there aren't any holes. Bake for 25 minutes, or until the edges begin to turn golden.

To make the lemon filling
Meanwhile, in a saucepan, whisk the eggs and sugar until well combined, then add the lemon juice and zest and gently whisk until completely combined. Gradually sift in the flour, whisking gently to combine, and add the butter. Heat the mixture, stirring constantly, until thick and the butter has melted.

Spoon the mixture over the warm crust, spread evenly to the edges and bake for 25 minutes, or until the edges begin to turn golden. The filling will firm up as it cools. Leave to cool completely in the pan, then dust with the icing sugar and cut into squares to serve.

Carrot, Parsnip and Coconut Flapjacks

Makes 12–16

100g/3½oz carrot
  (1 medium carrot), peeled
100g/3½oz parsnip
  (1 medium parsnip), peeled
150g/5oz/1½ cups rolled oats
50g/1¾oz/⅔ cup
  unsweetened desiccated
  (shredded) coconut
75g/2½oz/½ cup raisins, or
  other chopped dried fruit

4 tsp mixed seeds (linseeds,
  chia, pumpkin, sunflower or
  whatever you have to hand)
1 tsp ground cinnamon
125g/4½oz/½ cup
  salted butter
80g/3oz/heaped ⅓ cup light
  soft brown sugar
3 tbsp golden (corn) syrup
  or honey

Flapjacks are serious comfort food, from the moment the scent of the cinnamon wafts through the air as the oaty treats cool in their pan. They're also a great way to use up leftover packets of dried fruit, seeds or nuts (feel free to throw a handful of chopped nuts into the mixture).

Tip
—

We all have our favourite type of flapjacks. These ones are chewy with crispy edges, but if you like them crispier, then spread them a bit more thinly in a larger pan and turn the heat up to 190°C/ 170°C fan/375°F/gas 5.

Preheat the oven to 180°C/160°C fan/350°F/gas 4 and grease and line a 23cm/9in square cake pan with baking parchment.

Grate the carrot and parsnip and place in a large bowl with the oats, coconut, raisins, seeds and cinnamon, then stir to combine.

In a saucepan over a medium heat, gently melt the butter, sugar and syrup together, then pour it over the oat mixture and stir well.

Pour the mixture into the prepared pan, spread to the edges and press down firmly with the back of a spoon. Bake for about 35–40 minutes, or until the edges begin to turn brown.

Leave to cool completely in the pan and then cut into squares or bars.

Courgette and Chocolate Traybake with Cream Cheese Icing

Makes 16

250g/9oz courgette (zucchini) (1 medium courgette)
150g/5¼oz/¾ cup granulated sugar
125ml/4fl oz/generous ½ cup milk
75ml/2½fl oz/⅓ cup vegetable oil
75ml/2½fl oz/⅓ cup plain Greek yogurt
3 large free-range eggs
1 tsp vanilla extract
325g/11½oz/3 cups plain (all-purpose) flour
2 tsp baking powder
½ tsp salt

150g/5¼oz/¾ cup milk chocolate, roughly chopped
60g/2oz/generous ½ cup walnuts, roughly chopped
butter, for greasing

For the cream cheese icing
—
115g/4oz/½ cup soft cream cheese
4 tbsp butter, softened
200g/7oz/1⅔ cups icing (confectioners') sugar
1 tsp vanilla extract

To decorate
—
3 tbsp chopped walnuts

Courgettes (zucchini) are one of the vegetables that I am asked about the most – so many people seem to have gluts of them from the garden or the allotment and struggle to find ways to use them up. Growing up in Canada, courgette cake was just as popular as carrot cake. Usually made with chocolate chips – as I have done here – it was one of the most ubiquitous vegetable desserts. As the trend for putting veggies into cakes has gathered apace, it's nice to see the popularity of courgette cakes finally growing in the UK. Mine is a classic recipe dressed up with a cream cheese icing and a sprinkle of walnuts.

Preheat the oven to 180°C/160°C fan/350°F/gas 4. Lightly grease and line a 23cm/9in square baking pan.

Coarsely grate the unpeeled courgette, then place it into a clean tea towel and squeeze out any excess moisture.

In a large bowl, whisk the sugar, milk, oil, yogurt, eggs and vanilla. Sift in the flour, baking powder and salt, and mix. Add the courgette, chocolate and walnuts, and combine.

Pour the mixture into the prepared pan and bake for 40 minutes, or until the top is golden and a skewer inserted in the middle comes out clean.

Leave the cake to cool in the pan for 10 minutes, then transfer to a wire rack to cool completely before icing.

To make the cream cheese icing
Beat the cheese and butter with an electric mixer until smooth. Add the icing sugar and vanilla, and beat again until smooth and combined. Spread evenly over the top of the cooled cake, then cut into squares.

Beetroot Seedy Squares

Makes 16

200g/7oz cooked
  beetroot (roasted, boiled
  or steamed)
150g/5¼oz/⅔ cup
  pitted dates
150g/5¼oz/1½ cups
  rolled oats

215g/7½oz/1½ cup unsalted
  mixed seeds (linseeds,
  pumpkin, sesame,
  sunflower, chia, etc.)
3 tbsp coconut oil
½ tsp vanilla extract
butter, for greasing
1 tbsp pumpkin seeds,
  to decorate

My morning porridge gets a sprinkling of mixed seeds and they are lovely to nibble straight from the jar, so I tend to stock up on them regularly and always have plenty in the pantry – a great excuse for baking this recipe. You can use whichever seeds you have, buy bags of mixed seeds, or just add a little of this and that. I used chia, linseeds, pumpkin, hemp and sunflower seeds. These dense and chewy energy bars will keep you going for hours – and you don't even have to cook them. They are great for a quick, filling breakfast, or as a snack to get over through the afternoon slump. They're gently sweet from the dates, with an earthy beetroot flavour that comes through nicely.

Tip
—

You can save time by using pre-cooked vacuum-sealed beetroot, provided it's not packed in vinegar.

Grease a 20cm/8in square baking pan.

Soak the dates in warm water for 10 minutes, then drain and discard the water. Mix the seeds together in a bowl.

Whiz the beetroot, dates, oats, half the seeds and the coconut oil in a food processor until thick and well combined. Tip into the bowl with the remaining seeds, then mix well.

Press the mixture into the prepared pan, sprinkle with the pumpkin seeds and freeze for 1 hour. Remove and cut into squares. Store in the fridge.

Black Bean Chocolate Brownies

Makes 9–12

400g/15oz can black beans, drained and rinsed (215g/7oz drained weight)
100ml/3½fl oz/scant ½ cup vegetable oil, plus extra for greasing
2 large free-range eggs
50g/1¾oz/½ cup unsweetened cocoa powder
100g/3½oz/½ cup light soft brown sugar
2 tsp vanilla extract
1 tsp instant coffee granules
50g/1¾oz/heaped ⅓ cup plain (all-purpose) flour
½ tsp baking powder
½ tsp sea salt
50g/1¾oz good-quality dark chocolate, chopped
50g/1¾oz/½ cup walnuts, roughly chopped

We all love easy recipes, and for these brownies you just need to whiz everything up in the food processor, pour it into the pan and bake. I know that black bean brownies may seem even more bizarre than some of my other bakes, but the use of beans in brownies has been an internet sensation for a few years now, and rightly so. I've tweaked this recipe many times in order to get it just right. It's dense and fudgy, slightly crumbly and so decadently rich, with the beans providing bulk and fibre. The subtle addition of coffee enhances the chocolate, making the flavour even more rich.

Preheat the oven to 170°C/150°C fan/325°F/gas 3. Lightly grease and line a 20cm/8in square baking tin.

Purée the beans in a food processor. Add the oil, eggs, cocoa powder, sugar, vanilla and coffee, and blend until very smooth. Add the flour, baking powder and salt, then pulse a few times to combine. Stir in the chopped chocolate and half of the chopped walnuts.

Pour the batter into the prepared pan and spread out to level, then top with the remaining walnuts. Bake in the oven for 15–20 minutes, or until the edges begin to pull away from the sides and the surface begins to look dry.

Leave to cool completely in the pan before turning out and cutting into squares to serve.

Carrot Gingerbread

Makes 20

200g/7oz/scant 1 cup
  unsalted butter, plus extra
  for greasing
200g/7oz/scant 1 cup light
  soft brown sugar
200g/7oz/⅔ cup black
  treacle (molasses)
375g/13oz/3 cups plain
  (all-purpose) flour
3 tsp ground ginger

2 tsp bicarbonate of soda
  (baking soda)
250ml/8½fl oz/1 cup
  whole milk
150g/5¼oz carrot
  (1½ medium carrots,
  peeled)
2 large free-range eggs,
  beaten
3 pieces of stem ginger
  in syrup, chopped

These chunky slabs of gingerbread are rich, dark and elegantly spiced. I've added lots of grated carrot to make them extra moist, and it blends beautifully with the treacle and ginger. Although this old-fashioned classic takes a while in the oven, it is very easy to make.

For extra decadence, serve the gingerbread with hot custard, although a dollop of whipped cream or vanilla ice cream would also team up very well.

Preheat the oven to 160°C/140°C fan/320°F/gas 2. Grease and line a 23 x 30mm/9 x 12in baking pan with baking parchment.

Heat the butter, sugar and treacle in a pan, stirring, until smooth and melted. Leave to cool slightly.

Sift the flour, ginger and bicarbonate of soda into a large bowl. Stir in the milk, carrot, beaten egg, stem ginger and treacle mixture and stir to combine. Pour the mixture into the prepared pan and bake for 1 hour until well risen and springy in the middle.

Leave to cool in the pan for a few minutes, then turn out onto a wire rack to cool completely before cutting into squares.

Pies
+
Pastries

Mascarpone Tart with Beetroot Pastry

Serves 8

For the beetroot pastry
—

100g/3½oz raw beetroot
    (1 small beet), peeled
225g/8oz/1¾ cups plain
    (all-purpose) flour,
    plus extra for dusting
40g/1¼oz/⅓ cup icing
    (confectioners') sugar
1 pinch of salt
115g/4oz/½ cup cold
    unsalted butter,
    cut into cubes
1 tbsp cold water, if needed

For the filling
—

160ml/5¼fl oz/⅔ cup
    double (heavy) cream
200g/7oz white chocolate,
    chopped
400g/14oz/1¾ cup
    mascarpone cheese

To serve
—

fresh raspberries
grated white chocolate

The vibrant colour of beetroot cooks out of most bakes, but because chilled tarts have a short cooking time, the purple in this flaky buttery pastry doesn't have enough time to fade. This lovely pink crust holds a velvety-smooth mascarpone and white chocolate filling. It's rich, decadent and creamy, and perfectly offset by the sharp, fresh raspberries.

To make the pastry
Whiz the beetroot in a food processor until fine. Transfer to a bowl and set aside.

If you are making the pastry by hand, sift the flour, sugar and salt into a large bowl. Add the butter and use your fingertips to rub the butter into the flour mixture until it resembles breadcrumbs. Add the beetroot and mix with a knife until it forms a loose dough (add a tablespoon of cold water sparingly, if needed), then knead lightly until smooth.

Alternatively, to make the pastry in a food processor, pulse the flour, icing sugar, salt and butter until the mixture resembles fine breadcrumbs. Add the beetroot and pulse to combine. If the dough is too dry, add a tablespoon of very cold water until the dough comes together in a ball. Alternatively, if the dough is too wet, add a tablespoon of flour and pulse to combine.

Wrap the dough in cling film (plastic wrap) and chill for 30 minutes.

Preheat the oven to 180°C/160°C fan/350°F/gas 4 and lightly grease a 23cm/9in loose-bottomed pie dish.

Continued

Roll the dough out on a lightly floured surface and then line the pie dish with the pastry. Gently press it into the flutes and trim the edges by rolling the rolling pin over the edge. Refrigerate the pastry case for 15 minutes.

Line the base of the pastry case with parchment and cover the base with baking beans (or uncooked rice). Bake for 12 minutes, then remove the beans and parchment and cook for another 7 minutes, or until just starting to turn golden. Leave to cool.

To make the filling

Heat the cream until it just comes to the boil. Remove from the heat, add the chocolate, then let it stand for 2 minutes. Add the mascarpone and whisk until smooth. Fill cooled tart cases with the white chocolate mixture and refrigerate for 2 hours, or until the filling is firm. Top with raspberries and grated white chocolate and serve cold.

Butternut Squash and Ginger Hand Pies

Makes 8–10

For the pastry
—
340g/12oz/2¾ cups plain
(all-purpose) flour,
plus extra for dusting
3 tbsp caster (superfine) sugar
1 pinch of salt
200g/7oz/scant 1 cup cold
butter, cut into small cubes
2 large free-range egg yolks
3 tbsp very cold water

For the squash and
ginger filling
—
150g/5¼oz peeled butternut
squash, grated
2 apples, peeled, cored
and diced
75g/2½oz/½ cup raisins
50g/1¾oz/¼ cup crystallized
ginger, chopped
4 tbsp light soft brown sugar
1½ tsp cornflour (cornstarch)
1 tsp lemon juice
1 tsp ground cinnamon

To assemble
—
1 large free-range egg, beaten
2 tbsp demerara sugar
(or other coarse sugar)

These little hand pies are filled with a fragrant and spicy mix of grated butternut squash, apples, raisins and crystallized ginger. The squash adds bulk and a nutty sweetness to complement the tartness of the apples, while the small chunks of crystalized ginger chunks add bursts of spicy flavour alongside the plump warm raisins. Make these hand pies into any shape you like: cutting them into circles and folding will give them more of a traditional small pasty shape. The pies are lovely on their own or served warm with a scoop of vanilla ice cream.

To make the pastry
Sift the flour, sugar and salt into a large bowl. Add the butter and use your fingertips to rub the butter into the flour mixture until it resembles breadcrumbs.

In a separate bowl, mix the egg yolks and water, then add to the flour mixture. Mix with a butter knife until it forms a loose dough (add more cold water sparingly, if needed). Knead until smooth.

Alternatively, make in a food processor: add the flour, sugar, salt and butter to the bowl of the food processor. Pulse until it forms small crumbs. Mix the yolks and water and add to the food processor. Whiz until it all comes together in a ball.

Press the dough into a flat disc, wrap in cling film (plastic wrap) and refrigerate for at least 30 minutes.

Preheat the oven to 190°C/170°C fan/375°F/gas 5. Line two baking sheets with parchment paper.

Continued

If you want to tuck into these warm slices of fragrant fruit and veg and make this recipe a little quicker, feel free to use store-bought shortcrust pastry.

On a floured surface, roll the dough out thinly, to about 2mm thick and cut out about ten 15cm/6in squares, then place the squares on the prepared baking sheet. Re-roll and repeat with any remaining dough. Place the baking sheets of pastry squares into the fridge to chill while preparing the filling.

To make the squash and ginger filling
In a saucepan over a medium-low heat, combine the butternut squash, apples, raisins, crystallized ginger, sugar, cornflour, lemon juice and cinnamon, and heat gently for 5 minutes, stirring often so it doesn't scorch.

To assemble and finish
Remove the dough from the fridge and brush the edges with the beaten egg. Spoon 2 heaped teaspoons of the filling onto one side of each pastry square, fold the dough over, and use a fork to crimp and seal the edges. Brush with the egg, then use a sharp knife to cut slits in the pastry. Sprinkle with the demerara sugar and bake for 20–25 minutes, or until golden. Serve warm or cold.

Carrot Meringue Pie

Serves 6–8

For the pastry
—
170g/6oz/1⅓ cups plain
  (all-purpose) flour,
  plus extra for dusting
2 tbsp caster
  (superfine) sugar
1 pinch of salt
100g/3½oz/¼ cup cold butter,
  cut into small cubes,
  plus extra for greasing
1 large free-range egg yolk
2 tbsp very cold water

For the carrot filling
—
240ml/8fl oz/1 cup fresh
  carrot juice
zest and juice of 1 lemon
60g/2oz/½ cup cornflour
  (cornstarch)
250ml/9fl oz/1 cup water
200g/7oz/scant 1 cup caster
  (superfine) sugar
6 large free-range egg yolks

For the meringue topping
—
6 large free-range egg whites
200g/7oz/scant 1 cup caster
  (superfine) sugar
2 tsp cornflour (cornstarch)

Crowned with the traditional marshmallow meringue halo, this retro classic deserves to make a return to favour. When I was growing up, every restaurant and café seemed to feature a billowing lemon meringue pie on its menu, all their chefs competing to see who could pile their meringue the highest. Now nearing extinction, it's time to remember this airy showstopper.

Although I've made it with carrot, there's no getting around the fact that this pie is indulgent. Based on one that my parents used to make, it includes a sharp, lemony carrot curd that's zingy enough to contrast with the sweet meringue without being too sharp. I think it's best enjoyed alongside a glass of Babycham and a soundtrack of 1970s glam rock.

To make the pastry
Grease a 20cm/8in loose-bottomed pie pan.

Sift the flour, sugar and salt into a large bowl. Add the butter and use your fingertips to rub the butter into the flour mixture until it resembles breadcrumbs.

In a separate bowl, mix the egg yolks and water, then add to the butter mixture. Mix with a butter knife until it forms a loose dough (adding more cold water sparingly, if needed), then knead until smooth.

Alternatively, make in a food processor: add the flour, sugar, salt and butter to the bowl of the food processor. Pulse until it forms small crumbs. Mix the yolks and water and add to the food processor. Whiz until it all comes together in a ball.

On a floured surface, roll out the dough to 3mm/⅛ in thick and use it to line the prepared 20cm/8in pie pan. Place in the fridge and chill for 30 minutes.

Continued

Preheat the oven to 170°C/150°C fan/325°F/gas 3.

Line the base of the pastry case with baking parchment and fill with baking beans (or uncooked rice), then bake for 15 minutes. Remove the baking beans and parchment, then cook for another 5 minutes, or until just starting to turn golden. Set aside to make the filling, but leave the oven on.

To make the carrot filling
Drain the carrot juice through a muslin (cheesecloth) or sieve (fine-mesh strainer) and discard the pulp.

Mix the lemon juice and cornflour in a cup to form a paste.

In a saucepan, add the carrot juice, lemon zest and water and bring to the boil. Mix a few tablespoons of the hot carrot mixture into the lemon and cornflour mixture and stir until smooth, then pour this back into the pan and whisk until thick. Remove it from the heat and set aside.

In a large bowl, whisk the sugar and egg yolks together to mix well (be sure to save the egg whites for the meringue), and then whisk them into the hot carrot mixture. Continue whisking over the heat until thick and hot.

Leave to cool in the pan for a few minutes, then pour into the baked pastry case and spread it out to level.

To make the meringue topping
In a large bowl, beat the egg whites with an electric mixer until soft peaks form. Add the sugar, a tablespoon at a time, until the meringue is stiff. Add the cornflour and gently fold in to combine.

Spoon the meringue onto the pie to completely cover the filling. Use the back of the spoon to create peaks and swirls. Bake for 15 minutes, or until the meringue starts to brown.

Leave to cool completely for at least an hour before serving.

Avocado Lime Tarts

Makes 12

For the bases
—

100g/3½oz/¾ cup
   pitted dates
100g/3½oz/1 cup
   unsalted walnuts
55g/2oz/¾ cup unsweetened
   desiccated (dried flaked)
   coconut
1 tbsp coconut oil
¼ tsp salt

For the avocado filling
—

2 ripe avocados, pitted
   and peeled
100g/3½oz/1 cup raw
   unsalted cashews, soaked
   in water for at least 4 hours
   or overnight
50g/1¾oz/¼ cup coconut oil,
   melted
3 tbsp lime juice
100g/3½oz/¼ cup honey or
   maple syrup
2 tsp lime zest

To decorate
—

1 tbsp unsweetened
   desiccated (dried flaked)
   coconut
2 tsp lime zest

These vegan no-bake avocado lime tarts are full of nourishing ingredients. The lime adds a zip to the creamy avocado and cashews in the rich and velvety filling. Although these tarts are simple to whiz together, they will need an hour in the freezer to firm up. You can store them in the freezer, if you like, and just pop them into the fridge 10 minutes before serving to let them thaw slightly.

To make the bases
Line a 12-cup muffin pan with paper cases.

Combine all the base ingredients in a food processor and whiz until the mixture comes together into a sticky meal. If necessary, add a teaspoon of water and process again. Press a heaped tablespoon of the mixture into the base of each muffin cup and press down firmly, then place in the freezer while making the filling.

To make the avocado filling
Whiz all the filling ingredients in a blender or food processor until smooth. Pour onto the bases, smooth the tops and sprinkle with coconut and lime zest. Transfer to the freezer for 1 hour, or until firm.

Place in the refrigerator for 10 minutes to soften before serving. If not eating right away, store in the freezer, then thaw slightly in the fridge before serving.

Pumpkin Pie with Chai Cream

Serves 6–8

For the pastry

—

170g/6oz/generous 1⅓ cup plain (all-purpose) flour, plus extra for dusting
2 tbsp caster (superfine) sugar
1 pinch of salt
100g/3½oz/scant ½ cup cold butter, cut into small cubes, plus extra for greasing
1 egg yolk
2 tbsp very cold water

For the pumpkin filling

—

425g/15oz can of pumpkin purée
350ml/12fl oz can of evaporated milk
140g/5oz/scant ⅔ cup granulated sugar
2 large free-range eggs
1 tsp ground cinnamon
½ tsp ground ginger
¼ tsp ground cloves
¼ tsp salt

For the chai cream

—

240ml/8fl oz/1 cup double (heavy) cream
1 tbsp icing (confectioners') sugar
¼ tsp ground cinnamon
⅛ tsp ground cardamom
⅛ tsp ground ginger
1 pinch of freshly ground black pepper

Growing up in Canada, where pumpkin pie is an autumn classic, the crisp pastry not only holds creamy, spiced pumpkin, but also years of memories for me. Whether for Thanksgiving or Christmas, it featured regularly and was always made with canned pumpkin. Although I've toyed with the recipe many times over the years, here I've gone back to the nostalgic classic that I grew up on. To dress it up a little, I've teamed it with a fragrant chai-spiced cream. I remember the first time I ever tasted a hot, milky chai tea. It was in a market on Vancouver's Granville Island. It was an explosion of flavours, with ginger, cardamom, cinnamon and a bit of black pepper all brought together in the most perfumed of drinks. I've been smitten with chai ever since.

To make the pastry

Grease a 20cm/8in pie pan. Sift the flour, sugar and salt into a large bowl. Add the butter and use your fingertips to rub it into the flour mixture until it resembles breadcrumbs.

In a separate bowl, mix the egg yolks and water, then add to the butter mixture. Mix with a butter knife until it forms a loose dough (add a little cold water sparingly, if required), then knead until smooth.

Alternatively, make in a food processor: add the flour, sugar, salt and butter to the bowl of the food processor. Pulse until it forms small crumbs. Mix the yolks and water and add to the food processor. Whiz until it all comes together in a ball.

On a floured surface, roll out the dough to 3mm/⅛ in thick and use it to line the prepared pie pan. Place in the fridge and chill for 30 minutes.

Preheat the oven to 200°C/180°C fan/400°F/gas 6.

Continued

You can make the pastry as below or use a package packet of store-bought shortcrust pastry.

Line the base of the pastry case with baking parchment and fill with baking beans (or uncooked rice), then bake for 7 minutes. Remove the baking beans and parchment, then cook for another 7 minutes, or until just starting to turn golden. Remove from the oven and leave to one side.

Reduce the oven temperature to 180°C/160°C fan/350°F/gas 4.

To make the pumpkin filling
In a large bowl, whisk all the filling ingredients until combined. Pour the custard into the pastry case and bake for 30–40 minutes until set but still slightly wobbly in the centre.

Leave to cool completely before serving, topped with the chai cream.

To make the chai cream
In a large bowl, beat all ingredients together until light and fluffy. Store in the fridge until ready to pipe or spoon on top of the pumpkin pie.

Parsnip and Apple Tarte Tatin

Serves 8

100g/3½oz/¼ cup butter
100g/3½oz/½ cup
  granulated sugar
6 eating (dessert) apples,
  peeled, cored and quartered

100g/3½oz parsnip
  (1 medium parsnip),
  peeled and grated
1 x 375g/13oz packet of
  ready-rolled puff pastry

The French classic brings together rich caramel, apples and crispy, flaky puff pastry, but for my version, I've also grated in sweet, nutty parsnip. You can use any type of eating (dessert) apples that you like, but I like to choose a mix of sweet and tart apple varieties. Tarte tatin can be made with either puff pastry or shortcrust. I prefer puff, but if you're not going to be eating it quickly, use shortcrust so it will keep for longer without turning soggy from the caramel. Use it in the same way as the puff pastry.

Tip
—

If you cut the apples ahead of time, put them into a bowl of cold water with a squeeze of lemon juice to stop them browning.

Preheat the oven to 200°C/180°C fan/400°F/gas 6.

Melt the butter in a 23cm/9in ovenproof frying pan over a medium heat, then stir in the sugar until it dissolves. Increase the heat and let it cook for 4–5 minutes until it forms a rich, dark caramel.

Carefully arrange the apple slices onto the hot caramel, core-sides up, then sprinkle with the grated parsnip.

Unroll the pastry and prick it with a fork a few times. Lay the pastry over the pan, trim away any excess and tuck in the edges down the sides – carefully as the pan will still be hot.

Bake for 25 minutes, or until the pastry is crisp and golden.

Remove from the oven and leave to cool for a few minutes. Run a knife around the edge to loosen the pastry, then place a plate over the tart and carefully flip to invert it onto the plate.

Frozen Desserts

Cucumber and Lemon Granita

Serves 4–6

500ml/17fl oz/generous
   2 cups water
250g/9oz/generous 1 cup
   caster (superfine) sugar
300g/10½oz cucumber
   (1 medium cucumber)
250ml/9fl oz/generous
   1 cup lemon juice
   (from about 5 lemons)

This refreshing granita combines sharp lemons with the fresh flavour of cucumber. Perfect for a hot summer's day, the icy crystals are bursting with flavour. At once a grown-up slush puppy or a frozen salad, either way, it's sweet and tangy, cooling and tart. With no need for an ice-cream maker, all you have to do is blend the cucumber and add it to sugared water with lemon juice, then run a fork through it regularly as it freezes to break up the ice.

Tip
—

Any leftover cucumber purée is lovely stirred into sparkling water with a squeeze of lemon, or added to a gin and tonic.

Put the water into a saucepan and bring to the boil. Add the sugar and stir until the sugar dissolves completely, then remove from the heat and allow it to cool, which will take about 30 minutes.

Peel the cucumber and cut in half lengthways. Running a teaspoon along the length, scoop out the seeds and discard. Cut the remaining cucumber into chunks and purée in a food processor or with a hand blender. Measure out 250ml/9fl oz of the cucumber purée and use the rest for something else (see Tip).

Combine the cucumber purée and lemon juice and press through a sieve (fine-mesh strainer) over a bowl to collect the juice. Add the cucumber lemon juice to the sugar syrup and stir. Pour the mixture into a shallow freezer container and freeze for 30 minutes, or until ice crystals form around the edges. Break up the ice crystals with a fork, then return to the freezer. Repeat every 30 minutes, 3–4 times until the granita is fluffy and completely made of ice crystals. Scrape into dishes to serve. If the granita becomes too firm before serving, allow it to soften in the fridge until you can scrape it again.

Beetroot and Vanilla Sorbet

Serves 4–6

300g/10½oz cooked beetroot
  (roasted, steamed or boiled)
150g/5¼oz/¾ cup caster
  (superfine) sugar
100g/3½fl oz/scant
  ½ cup water

The sweet, earthy beetroot flavour isn't masked in this sorbet, rather it shines alongside the vanilla. It makes a refreshing and eye-catching dessert – with its vivid purple colour – a dinner party palate-cleanser, or lovely in a cone on a hot summer's day. This sorbet is particularly easy to make in an ice-cream maker, but you can use a dish in the freezer if you don't have one.

Tip
—

The recipe works well with roasted, steamed or boiled beetroots, or even store-bought beetroots vacuum-packed in water.

If using an ice-cream maker, freeze the bowl ahead of time, according to the manufacturer's instructions.

Purée the beetroot with a hand blender until smooth, then set aside.

In a small saucepan over a medium-low heat, combine the sugar and water, stirring occasionally until completely dissolved. This could take about 5 minutes. Remove from the heat and leave to cool slightly.

In a food processor, blend the cooled sugar syrup with the puréed beetroot, lemon juice and vanilla until smooth.

If using an ice-cream maker, pour the cooled mixture into the pre-frozen bowl of the ice-cream maker and churn until thick, according to the manufacturer's instructions, then either serve immediately or pour into a freezer-safe dish to store in the freezer.

If not using an ice-cream maker, pour the cooled mixture into a large freezer-safe dish and freeze, mixing it well with a fork every half an hour over the next 4 hours. Transfer to the fridge for 15 minutes to soften before serving.

Chocolate Cauliflower Ice Lollies with Pistachio Dust

Makes 10–12

150g/5¼oz/½ cup cauliflower florets
400ml/14oz can of coconut milk
200g/7oz/1½ cups packed pitted soft dates
30g/1oz/¼ cup unsweetened cocoa powder

To decorate
—
35g/1¼ oz/¼ cup good-quality dark chocolate, melted
50g/1¾oz/⅓ cup shelled unsalted pistachios

We all know someone who says that they hate cauliflower, don't we? No wonder, when these poor brassicas are so often over-boiled. These rich and fudgy ice lollies – drizzled with melted chocolate and a sprinkling of pistachio dust – will banish any painful memories of bland cauliflower cheese.

These popsicles are fudgy, rich and almost mousse-like. The puréed cauliflower can't be tasted, but it adds nourishing bulk. The sweet, chocolatey lollies are drizzled with melted chocolate and a sprinkling of pistachio dust. Why? Just for a bit of pizazz. Cauliflower always deserves pizazz. They are pictured here with the Cucumber and Lemon Ice Lollies (recipe on p.116).

Steam the cauliflower over a pan of simmering water for a few minutes until just soft, then rinse under cold water to stop it cooking and drain well.

Soak the dates in warm water for 10 minutes to soften, then drain and discard the water.

Process the cauliflower, dates and all the other ice lolly ingredients in a food processor or blender until very smooth. Pour into moulds and freeze until solid.

To decorate
Melt the chocolate for a few seconds in a microwave or in a double boiler.

Process the pistachios in a mini food processor or food mill until they turn to fine crumbs. Drizzle the frozen lollies with the melted chocolate and sprinkle with the pistachio dust.

Cucumber and Lemon Ice Lollies

Makes 12

1 cucumber, skin on
juice of ½ lemon
1 tbsp lemon zest
250ml/9fl oz/generous
  1 cup water
1 tbsp honey or favourite
  sweetener

Pretty much a frozen salad on a stick, these healthy lollies are simplicity itself to make and taste vibrant, fresh and summery – the perfect way to cool down on hot days.

Pictured on p.114, along with the Chocolate Cauliflower Ice Lollies with Pistachio Dust.

Add all ingredients to a blender and blitz until smooth. Pour into ice lolly moulds and freeze until solid.

Sweetcorn and Coconut Ice Cream

Serves 4

250g/9oz/1 cup
  sweetcorn kernels
  (fresh or defrosted frozen)
400ml/14oz can of coconut
  cream, chilled in the fridge
  overnight or for at least
  3 hours
5 tbsp caster (superfine) sugar
2 tbsp coconut oil
2 tsp vanilla extract

To decorate
—
4 tsp unsweetened
  desiccated (dried flaked)
  coconut

Sweetcorn and coconut is a popular dessert flavour combination across the world. In Vietnam, the traditional *chè bắp* is a pudding made with tapioca, corn and coconut, while similar desserts are popular across South East Asia. In the Philippines, *maja blanca* is a gelatinous coconut milk pudding often made with corn that is popular during holidays, while the Mexican *atole* is a popular street-food drink of cashews, coconut water and sweetcorn.

This soft and creamy ice cream is a dreamy interpretation of this popular pairing. With only a few ingredients whizzed in a blender and then frozen, this simple dessert turns the humble kernel of corn into something special. You can use fresh corn in season, or frozen corn. It's easiest to make this with an ice-cream maker, but if you don't have one, you can freeze the ice cream in a container and then blitz it in a food processor.

If using an ice-cream maker, freeze the bowl ahead of time, according to the manufacturer's instructions.

Boil the sweetcorn kernels for a few minutes until cooked. Drain, run under cold water to cool, then drain again.

Transfer the sweetcorn to a blender or food processor, add the remaining ingredients and blitz until smooth. The coconut cream will have separated in the can, but use both the cream and the liquid. Chill the mixture in the fridge for 45 minutes.

Pour into the ice-cream maker and churn until thick, according to the manufacturer's instructions. Sprinkle with desiccated coconut and serve immediately as soft serve, or place in a freezer-proof dish and return to the freezer.

If you don't have an ice-cream maker, add the chilled mixture to a freezer-safe container and place in the freezer. Once every hour, remove from the freezer and stir briskly to incorporate air and disperse the ice crystals. Repeat every hour until firm (about 6 hours). Alternatively, allow it to freeze solid, then cut into chunks and purée in a food processor, then refreeze before serving.

If it is solid, transfer to the fridge 20 minutes before serving to let it soften enough to scoop.

Pumpkin and Almond Swirled Frozen Yogurt Bark

Serves 6

For the almond yogurt
—

250g/9oz/1 cup plain Greek
    yogurt
2 tbsp honey
¼ tsp almond extract
a little oil, for greasing

For the pumpkin swirl
—

3 tbsp pumpkin purée
    (canned, or purée cooked
    pumpkin or squash)
1 tbsp honey
¼ tsp ground cinnamon
⅛ tsp ground ginger
⅛ tsp freshly grated nutmeg

For the topping
—

2 tbsp unsalted whole
    almonds
1 tbsp unsalted flaked
    (slivered) almonds

Frozen yogurt bark is so easy to make, and it makes a lovely dessert or a rather special breakfast. The lightly spiced pumpkin is swirled around the almond-flavoured yogurt and then topped with nuts. You simply freeze it for a few hours and then chop it into shards. If you're not eating it right away, just store the shards of frozen yogurt in the freezer.

Tip
—

Although pumpkin purée is available in most supermarkets, you can easily make your own by puréeing cooked butternut squash or pumpkin with a hand blender.

To make the frozen yogurt
Lightly grease a shallow 20cm/8in square baking pan (or a size that fits in your freezer) and line with baking parchment.

Mix all of the almond yogurt ingredients, reserve 1 tablespoon to add to the pumpkin mixture and pour the rest evenly into the pan.

To make the pumpkin swirl
Mix all the pumpkin swirl ingredients and mix with the tablespoon of yogurt. Drop teaspoonfuls onto the yogurt then cut through with a knife to create swirls.

Top decoratively with the almonds, then freeze for at least 2 hours. Remove from the pan and chop into large shards. Enjoy immediately or store in the freezer. Transfer to the fridge for 15 minutes to soften before serving.

Avocado and Lime Ice Cream

Serves 4

2 ripe avocados, pitted
  and peeled
225ml/7½fl oz/scant 1 cup
  milk (dairy or non-dairy
  such as almond)
3–4 tbsp caster
  (superfine) sugar
juice of 1 lime

This very easy ice cream uses ripe avocado flesh as its base, and for this recipe I've included lime to give the smooth and creamy ice cream a South American flavour kick. You can make this vegan by using non-dairy milk (almond milk works well) and can steer clear of refined sugar by substituting maple syrup or honey for the caster (superfine) sugar. Instead of making a sugar syrup, I've simply whizzed the caster sugar with the other ingredients in the blender – so be sure to mix it up really well to eliminate any grit from the sugar.

Tip

—

Freeze the bowl of an ice-cream maker in advance. If you don't have one, just follow the instructions below.

Whiz all ingredients in a blender or food processor until smooth. Taste and adjust the sweetness, if necessary.

Pour into the ice-cream maker and churn according to the manufacturer's instructions.

Serve immediately or pour into a freezer-proof dish and freeze.

If you don't have an ice-cream maker, pour the cooled mixture into a large freezer-safe dish and freeze, whisking it every half hour over the next 4 hours. Put in the fridge for 15 minutes to soften before serving.

More Sweet Treats

Chocolate Beetroot Baked Doughnuts with Blueberry Glaze

Makes 12

For the doughnuts
—

150g/5¼oz cooked beetroot
(roasted, boiled or steamed)
125g/4½oz/⅔ cup granulated
sugar
250ml/9fl oz/generous
1 cup whole milk
1 large free-range egg
50g/1¾oz/¼ cup unsalted
butter, melted and cooled
2 tsp vanilla extract

250g/9oz/2 cups plain
(all-purpose) flour
4 tbsp unsweetened
cocoa powder
2 tsp baking powder
1 pinch of salt
a little oil, for greasing

For the blueberry glaze
—

150g/5¼oz/scant 1¼ cups
icing (confectioners') sugar
35g/1oz/¼ cup fresh
blueberries

Lately, beetroot and chocolate have become a hugely popular flavour combination, often featuring in cafés and restaurants in the form of brownies, cakes and cookies. It's not surprising; the sweet beetroot flavour adds a faint hint of earthiness beneath the deep, rich chocolate.

You'll need a doughnut pan for this recipe, but they're easy to source online. I don't tend to deep-fry at home, so discovering that you can bake doughnuts has meant that I can now make them myself, plus they're far less calorific when cooked in the oven. They are also very simple to make. I've topped them with a vibrant blueberry glaze, bringing both fruit and vegetables together in these pretty treats.

Tip
—

If you use vacuum-packed beetroot, make sure it is not in vinegar.

To make the doughnuts
Preheat the oven to 170°C/150°C fan/325°F/gas 3. Lightly grease a doughnut pan with oil.

Finely grate the cooked beetroot in a food processor. You can do this by hand, but it will be messy.

In a large bowl, beat the grated beetroot, sugar, milk, egg, cooled melted butter and vanilla together. Sift in the flour, cocoa powder, baking powder and salt, and gently combine.

Fill the doughnut moulds with the batter until nearly full and bake for 15 minutes, or until springy and a skewer inserted in the middle comes out clean.

Leave to cool in the pan for 5 minutes, then carefully transfer to a wire rack to cool completely.

To make the blueberry glaze
Whiz the blueberries and icing sugar with a hand blender or in a small food processor until smooth. It should be a thick drizzling consistency. If necessary, add a teaspoon more of icing (confectioners') sugar to thicken, or a few blueberries to thin, and whiz again. Drizzle over the completely cooled doughnuts.

Butternut Squash Cinnamon Rolls with Almond Glaze

Makes 8

For the rolls
—
250g/9oz/2 cups strong
   white bread flour,
   plus extra for dusting
½ tsp salt
1 sachet (7g/2 tsp) fast-action
   dry yeast
125ml/4¼fl oz/½ cup
   whole milk, plus extra
   for glazing
25g/1oz/⅛ cup unsalted
   butter
1 large free-range egg, beaten
a little oil, for greasing

For the squash and
raisin filling
—
100g/3½oz peeled and
   deseeded butternut squash,
   cut into chunks
50g/1¾oz/¼ cup unsalted
   butter, softened
50g/1¾oz/¼ cup light soft
   brown sugar
1½ tsp ground cinnamon
50g/1¾oz/⅓ cup raisins

For the almond glaze
—
70g/2½oz/½ cup icing
   (confectioners') sugar
1–2 tbsp whole milk
½ tsp almond extract

Superbly sticky with their almond glaze, these fruity cinnamon rolls just beckon to be enjoyed warm from the oven with a cup of tea. The yeasted dough doesn't take long to make, though it does need time on its own to rise. It's a soft dough, so expect it to stick to your fingers as you work, but it will soon come together smoothly enough to work into a ball. The dough is then filled with a spiral of cinnamon-spiced butternut squash, which adds a nutty aromatic sweetness, and finally dotted with plump raisins, great for dessert, a snack or a cheeky, decadent breakfast.

To make the dough
Pour the flour into a large bowl, then add the salt on one side and the yeast on the other. This is to stop the salt from possibly killing the yeast and affecting the rise.

In a small saucepan, gently heat the milk and butter until warm and the butter has melted.

Mix the flour with the yeast and salt (it's okay for them to touch now), make a well in the centre and pour in the warm milk and butter mixture, and the beaten egg. Stir to make a sticky dough.

With floured hands, knead the dough in the bowl (or on a lightly floured surface) for 5 minutes until it is smooth and elastic. It will be quite sticky, so add a small amount of flour, if necessary, to make it manageable. Alternatively, knead the dough in a stand mixer for 5 minutes until it's smooth and elastic.

Place the dough into a lightly oiled bowl, cover it with a tea towel and leave in a warm place for 45 minutes.

Continued

To make the filling

Steam the squash over a pan of boiling water until soft. Drain and purée with a hand blender, then set aside to cool.

Mix the butter and sugar together well, then stir in the cinnamon and cooled squash purée.

To make the rolls

Tip the dough onto a lightly floured surface and knead it a few times to knock it back. Roll it out with a floured rolling pin to 25 x 30cm/10 x 12in.

Lightly grease a 20cm/8in round cake pan.

Spread the filling over the dough, leaving a 2.5cm/1in border around the edges, then sprinkle it with the raisins. Roll the dough along the long side and cut the log in half, then cut each half into 4 to make 8 pieces. Place the rolls into the prepared pan cut-side facing up, with a little space between them to allow for expansion. Cover with a tea towel and leave in a warm place to rise for 30 minutes.

Preheat the oven to 190°C/170°C fan/375°F/gas 5.

Brush cinnamon rolls with a little milk and cook for 20–25 minutes, or until risen and golden.

To make the glaze

Mix the icing sugar, milk and almond extract in a bowl. Add small amounts of additional milk or sugar to reach a drizzling consistency.

Allow the rolls to cool in the pan slightly before drizzling with the almond glaze. Serve warm or cold.

Chocolate, Avocado and Orange Mousse with Spiced Orange Coconut Cream

Serves 4

For the chocolate mousse
—
8 dates, pitted (5 if using
   large Medjool dates)
1 ripe avocado, peeled
   and pitted
2½ tbsp unsweetened
   cocoa powder
juice of 1 orange
½ tsp orange zest
¼ tsp vanilla extract
⅛ tsp ground cinnamon

For the spiced orange
coconut cream
—
400ml/15oz can of
   coconut milk, chilled in
   the fridge overnight
1 tsp orange juice
½ tsp orange zest
⅛ tsp ground cinnamon
⅛ tsp freshly grated nutmeg

To decorate
—
Orange zest

The combination of chocolate and orange always reminds me of Christmas, but this intense and silky mousse is great at any time of year. It's easy to whip up and you can even make it a day ahead and keep it in the fridge. It's also vegan, gluten-free and refined sugar-free – but still decadent and delicious. For an extra grown-up treat, add a teaspoon of triple-sec orange liqueur to the mousse.

Tip

—

For the coconut cream, it's important that the coconut milk has been chilled overnight so that it will whip up. When using it, you only want to whip the thick cream that has separated from the water during chilling.

To make the mousse
Soak the pitted dates in warm water for 10 minutes to soften, then drain and discard the water.

Combine the dates with the avocado flesh, cocoa, orange juice and zest, vanilla and cinnamon in a blender or small food processor and whiz until smooth. Chill in the fridge for a few hours.

To make the spiced orange coconut cream
Pour the liquid from the tin of coconut milk and scoop the chilled coconut cream into a large bowl. Whip for a few minutes with an electric mixer until thick.

Add the orange zest and juice, as well as the spices, and beat to combine.

Top the chilled chocolate mousse with the coconut cream and orange zest. Serve chilled.

Sweet Potato and Fresh Ginger Balls with Coconut Dust

Makes 25

125g/4½oz/1¼ cups rolled oats
200g/7oz/scant 1 cup cooked
　sweet potato
　(1 medium sweet potato),
　mashed and cooled
125g/4⅓oz/½ cup smooth
　peanut butter
¼ tsp freshly grated ginger
　(or more to taste)
1 tbsp honey or maple syrup
½ teaspoon vanilla extract

To finish
—

3 tbsp desiccated
　(dried flaked) coconut

Sweet potato and fresh ginger taste so warm and autumnal together. I often cook jacket sweet potatoes and frequently roast a spare one so I can make these balls. Once the sweet potato is cooked, it takes only minutes to whiz these treats together. If you like a bit of heat, go ahead and add a little extra fresh ginger.

Tip
—

A perfect sweet snack, I also like to keep a stash of energy balls in the freezer and just grab a few each day for breakfast on the go.

Blitz the oats in a food processor to make them a bit finer, then add the remaining ingredients and process until combined. Taste and add more ginger if desired, then process again.

Whiz the coconut in a mini food processor until fine, then place in a flat bowl.

Roll the sweet potato mixture into teaspoon-sized balls, then roll in the coconut and store in the refrigerator.

Cauliflower and Chocolate Hazelnut Filo Sticks with Cinnamon Sugar

Makes 12

100g/3½oz/⅔ cup unsalted hazelnuts
150g/5¼oz/¾ cup mashed steamed cauliflower
4 tbsp icing (confectioners') sugar
2 tbsp unsweetened cocoa powder
½ tsp vanilla extract
⅛ tsp salt
250g/9oz package of filo pastry sheets, thawed
60g/2oz/generous ¼ cup butter, melted

For dusting (optional)
—
3 tbsp caster (superfine) sugar
1 tsp ground cinnamon

These delicately crunchy filo sticks, fragrant from the cinnamon sugar, are filled with a homemade chocolate hazelnut spread made with puréed cauliflower, giving a creamy and rich result.

Tip
—
The more powerful your blender, the quicker you will be able to make the nut butter. These are best eaten straight away so the pastry remains crisp.

Preheat the oven to 180°C/160°C fan/350°F/gas 4.

Place the hazelnuts on a baking sheet and roast for 8–10 minutes, or until lightly toasted. Transfer them to a tea towel and, when they're cool enough to handle, rub the skins off with the tea towel. They won't all come off, but just try to get as much as possible.

Place the hazelnuts into a small food processor and process for about 10 minutes, or until they form a thick nut butter. You'll need to scrape the sides down frequently and the mixture will turn crumbly, then sandy, then the nuts will release their oils and turn into a creamy nut butter. Keep processing to get it as smooth as possible.

When the nut butter is ready, add the mashed cauliflower, along with all the other ingredients and process until smooth, scraping the sides down regularly as needed. Taste for sweetness and add more icing sugar, if necessary. Spoon the mixture into a piping bag and refrigerate until ready to use.

Preheat the oven or increase the oven temperature to 200°C/180°C fan/400°F/gas 6. Line a baking sheet with baking parchment.

Continued

More Sweet Treats

Keep the filo sheets that you aren't using under a slightly damp tea towel so they don't dry out. Brush a sheet of filo pastry with butter, then place another sheet on top and brush it with butter as well. Cut the stack of two filo sheets into four rectangles of equal size.

On each double-layer strip, leaving a small gap at the top and bottom, pipe the cauliflower chocolate mixture along the length on one side, then tuck the ends in and roll it into a cigar shape. Place it on the baking sheet and repeat with the other strips and sheets.

Bake the filo rolls for 12 minutes, or until they turn crisp and golden. Mix the cinnamon and sugar on a plate, then roll the hot filo sticks in it. Serve warm or cold.

More Sweet Treats

Parsnip and Plum Crumble with Gingerbread Topping

Serves 6

For the plum filling
—

200g/7oz parsnip (2 medium parsnips), peeled
500g/1lb 2oz/3 cups plums, pitted and quartered
1 tbsp granulated sugar
1 tbsp plain (all-purpose) flour

For the gingerbread topping
—

100g/3½oz/generous ¾ cup plain (all-purpose) flour
70g/2½oz/⅓ cup demerara sugar (or granulated)
½ tsp ground cinnamon
½ tsp ground ginger
¼ tsp ground allspice
⅛ tsp freshly grated nutmeg
⅛ tsp ground cloves
75g/2½oz/⅓ cup cold unsalted butter, cubed

The tartness of the plums tastes lovely next to the subtly sweet parsnip in this winter-warmer. The crumble topping has all the flavours of gingerbread, so it smells absolutely dreamy while it's cooking, and tastes even better. This comforting crumble is perfect on its own or with custard or ice cream, and is a great end to a Sunday roast lunch.

Tip
—

I've used demerara sugar in the topping, which gives it a lovely bit of crunch. Feel free to substitute it with granulated sugar if you don't like the extra texture or if you don't have any to hand.

To make the plum filling
Preheat the oven to 180°C/160°C fan/350°F/gas 4.

Grate the parsnip and place it, along with the plums, into a 23 x 33cm/9 x 13in ovenproof dish. Sprinkle the flour and sugar over the plums and parsnips, mixing until coated.

To make the gingerbread topping
In a large bowl, mix the flour, sugar and spices together. With fingertips, rub the butter into the spiced flour until it resembles breadcrumbs. Sprinkle over the filling and bake for 40 minutes, or until golden. Serve warm or cold.

Sweet Potato Dessert Waffles

Serves 6

250g/9oz/2 cups plain
  (all-purpose) flour
5 tbsp light soft brown sugar
1 tsp baking powder
½ tsp bicarbonate of soda
  (baking soda)
1 pinch of salt
1 tsp ground cinnamon
½ tsp ground ginger
½ tsp ground cloves
¼ tsp freshly grated nutmeg
200g/7oz/1½ cup mashed
  cooked sweet potato
  (steamed or roasted)
3 large free-range eggs
300ml/10½fl oz/1¼ cups milk
3 tbsp butter, melted

To serve (optional)
—
vanilla ice cream
chocolate sauce
mixed nuts, roughly chopped
sprinkles

Waffles shouldn't be consigned only to the breakfast table. With the addition of sweet potato and spices, these are perfect served warm with a scoop of vanilla ice cream, ready to melt into its waffley pockets. My kids love waffles and call them Lego pancakes – they're so easy to make and absolutely delicious. A waffle maker isn't the most necessary of gadgets, but it's one that we love to pull out at the weekends to make an extra-special breakfast together – or indeed to use for these quick dessert waffles.

Tip
—

These are a great way to use up leftover sweet potato and or you could also substitute leftover mashed potato or butternut squash.

Preheat the waffle iron.

In a large bowl, whisk together the flour, brown sugar, baking powder, bicarbonate of soda, spices and salt.

In another bowl, whisk the mashed sweet potato, eggs, milk and melted butter.

Pour the wet mixture into the flour mixture and stir to combine.

Cook the waffles in batches in the waffle iron, according to the manufacturer's instructions.

Serve the waffles topped with scoops of ice cream, chocolate sauce, nuts and sprinkles, as desired.

More Sweet Treats

Chocolate Aubergine Truffles

Makes about 20

150g/5¼oz aubergine
200ml/7fl oz/scant 1 cup
   double (heavy) cream
1 tbsp caster (superfine) sugar
200g/7oz/¾ cup good-quality
   dark chocolate, chopped
50g/1¾oz/⅓ cup
   unsweetened cocoa powder,
   for dusting

Aubergine brings a wonderfully deep, slightly bitter underlying flavour to these rich chocolate truffles. You might consider aubergine another particularly unusual vegetable to pair with chocolate, but it is a common combination in some parts of the world, such as in Naples, where *Melanzane al Cioccolato* is a very popular dessert made with layers of aubergine, ricotta and chocolate. Truffles are so easy to make, as long as you don't mind getting your hands dirty. I find the rolling quite therapeutic and my kids love to help as well.

Cut the aubergine into chunks and steam until soft. Drain well, then purée with a hand blender. Transfer the purée to a saucepan and heat gently for a few minutes, stirring constantly, to remove the excess moisture. It's ready when the moisture stops sizzling in the pan. Place the aubergine purée into a bowl, then pour the chopped chocolate on top, but don't stir them together.

In a saucepan, gently heat the cream and sugar until it is just about to reach the point of boiling.

Pour the hot cream over the chocolate and leave for 1 minute, then stir well until it's smooth and the chocolate, aubergine and cream are all combined. Refrigerate for a few hours until firm.

Roll a teaspoonful of the truffle mix into a ball with your hands and then roll in the cocoa to coat. Repeat with the rest of the mixture. Store the truffles in the fridge until ready to serve.

Sparkling Carrot Lemonade

Makes 1 litre/1¾ pints

450g/1lb carrots, peeled
3 lemons, peeled
10g/½oz/½in ginger, peeled
2 handfuls of ice
750ml/25fl oz/3 cups
  sparkling water
caster (superfine) sugar, to
  sweeten (optional)

This refreshing and tangy lemonade is so luminously bright, it's like a 1990s rave drink. You can add a teaspoon of caster (superfine) sugar if desired, but I find that it doesn't need it – the carrots sweeten it naturally.

Juice the carrots, lemons and ginger in a juicer. Add to a jug with the ice and top up with sparkling water. Taste and stir in caster sugar, if necessary.

Tip
—

This recipe is easiest in a juicer, but if you don't have one, whiz the carrots, lemon and ginger in a blender, then strain out the pulp over a bowl through a fine-mesh sieve (strainer), muslin (cheesecloth) or nut milk bag.

Index

Acknowledgements

I'd like to thank my husband, Marc, for all of his endless support, for encouraging me to follow my dream of writing a cookbook, for sampling all of my desserts and for always making me laugh.

To my little taste testers, Dax and Polly. You've been living every kid's dream, coming home to huge piles of cake every day. Sorry, but it's carrot sticks from now on. Thanks for your thumbs up/thumbs down and brutally honest opinions. You two are everything.

To my mum, for looking after my little ones so I could hurl flour about my kitchen in frenzied baking sessions. For giving them so much love, attention and time. For moving to be close to us and being such a huge part of our lives. It really means so much to us all.

To all of my friends and family, for all of your support with my blog, baking and this book.

A huge thank you to my wonderful agent, Amanda Preston at LBA, who has made this all happen and believed in me from the start.

Thank you to Ione for giving me this amazing opportunity and guiding me through this exciting process, and to Emily for seeing this book through with me.

To the photography team for bringing my recipes to life. To Clare Winfield for the stunning pictures, Emily Kydd for her wizardry with styling, Wei Tang for her gorgeous props, and everyone who helped at the shoots.

Thank you to the team at Pavilion, including Katie, Tory, Laura, Clare Clewley for design, and everyone else for bringing my dream to life.

Last but certainly not least, I'd like to give a heartfelt thank you to all of my blog readers. Your support over the past few years has meant so much to me.

Thank you all. This book couldn't have happened without you.

Kate xx

Blog: www.veggiedesserts.co.uk
Instagram: @kateveggiedesserts
Twitter: @veggie_desserts
Facebook: VeggieDessertsBlog

About the Author

Author of the award-winning website www.veggiedesserts.co.uk, Kate Hackworthy is a columnist for *Vegetarian Living* magazine and a regular contributor to Metro.co.uk. She has been featured in the mainstream press including the *Guardian*, *Cosmopolitan* and *Grazia*. Kate works with various high-profile brands as an ambassador, and counts Nigella Lawson, Jamie Oliver and Fearne Cotton among her followers. She lives in Somerset with her young family.